Praise for Jennifer

'Worth is indeed a natural storyteller term, with apparent artlessness in fa and her detailed account of being a m........ London's East End is gripping, moving and convincing from beginning to end . . . *Call the Midwife* is also a powerful evocation of a long-gone world . . . and in Worth it has surely found one of its best chroniclers'   David Kynaston, *Literary Review*

'Worth is a vivid writer with a talent for the sting in the tail'
Evening Standard

'Jennifer Worth has a gift for storytelling and a keen eye for the evocative'   BBC TV's *Who Do You Think You Are?*

'Worth's book made me cry in a railway carriage'
Matthew Parris, *Spectator*

'These are powerful stories delivered with sweet charm and controlled outrage'   *Times Literary Supplement*

'Worth's books are full of fascinating social history: about living conditions in east London, the scale of poverty and violence, the realities of postwar medicine and the workhouse'
New Statesman

'A chilling insight into life for the average mother [in the 1950s]'   *Sunday Express*

'There are desperately sad stories here, but tales of great hope too. Of ordinary people living, giving birth and building their families despite enormous hardship and poor sanitation. And of midwives delivering superb care in the toughest conditions'
...st End Life

9112000020 7398

Jennifer Worth trained as a nurse at the Royal Berkshire Hospital, Reading, and was later ward sister at the Elizabeth Garrett Anderson Hospital in London, then the Marie Curie Hospital, also in London. Music had always been her passion, and in 1973 she left nursing in order to study music intensively, teaching piano and singing for about 25 years. Jennifer died in May 2011 after a short illness, leaving her husband Philip, two daughters and three grandchildren. Her books have all been bestsellers.

By Jennifer Worth

Call the Midwife
Shadows of the Workhouse
Farewell to the East End
In the Midst of Life
Letters to the Midwife

Letters to the Midwife

Correspondence with the author of
Call the Midwife

With an introduction by
Philip Worth, Suzannah Hart
and Juliette Walton
and a foreword by Miranda Hart

Includes previously unpublished writing
by Jennifer Worth

PHOENIX

A PHOENIX PAPERBACK

First published in Great Britain in 2014
by Weidenfeld & Nicolson
This paperback edition published in 2014
by Phoenix,
an imprint of Orion Books Ltd,
Orion House, 5 Upper St Martin's Lane,
London WC2H 9EA

An Hachette UK company

1 3 5 7 9 10 8 6 4 2

Excerpt 'The Paris Interlude', Jennifer Worth's journal entries
and letters © Estate of Jennifer Worth 2014

Introduction copyright © Philip Worth, Suzannah Hart
and Juliette Walton 2014

Foreword © Kingmaker Productions Limited 2014

A CIP catalogue record for this book
is available from the British Library.

ISBN 978-1-7802-2464-0

Printed and bound by CPI Group (UK) Ltd, Croydon CR0 4YY

The Orion Publishing Group's policy is to use papers that
are natural, renewable and recyclable products and made
from wood grown in sustainable forests. The logging and
manufacturing processes are expected to conform to the
environmental regulations of the country of origin.

www.orionbooks.co.uk

This book is dedicated to the memory of
Jennifer Worth whose life and work are
an inspiration to so many

Contents

Acknowledgements

We would like to thank Pat Birch, Brenda Fleming, Sarah Garrett and Jackie Horne for filling in certain details of family background. Special thanks to Lydia and Eleanor Hart and Daniel Hartworth for their childhood memories.

Also, Lisa Edwards at the Centre for Buckinghamshire Studies for assistance with local history and Richard Grylls for his genealogical expertise.

Finally, we would like to thank everyone who wrote to Jennifer and whose letters inspired this book.

Foreword

For those of you who have read *Call the Midwife* you will know that Jennifer Worth creates the most wonderful imagery with her writing. She portrayed such vivid pictures of an extraordinary time in British history and of truly extraordinary women in the midwives who devoted years to their vocation and saved many women's lives. Midwifery and women's health truly mattered to them and they were, in my view, heroines.

I owe Jennifer an awful lot. She wrote to me in 2010, sent me a copy of her book and told me that I reminded her of her friend Chummy and if *Call the Midwife* ever got made into a television series she would be thrilled if I played the part. I immediately turned to Chummy's entrance in the book and fell in love with how she portrayed this clumsy woman appearing at Nonnatus House in the East End – a fish out of water determined to follow her heart's desire and do herself proud. I knew I had to play the part. And I will always be incredibly grateful to her for the opportunity.

Sadly, I never got to meet Jennifer. I wish I had. To have been able to thank her. But here we are lucky enough to have further insight into her life through her correspondence and a chance to wallow happily in her beautiful writing. Thank you, Jennifer.

Miranda Hart

Note

Jennifer Worth was a beloved wife, mother, grandmother, sister, aunt and cousin. She was a friend to so many, but she was Jennifer to all. This is how we will refer to her throughout the introduction.

Jennifer Worth – a truly remarkable woman

The young Jennifer

Many adjectives come to mind when describing Jennifer Worth. She was kind, caring and loving, highly creative, incredibly generous, single-minded, slightly eccentric and always surprising.

Even the circumstances surrounding her birth are something of a surprise. Little is clear but what is certain is that her mother and grandmother were staying in Clacton during the latter part of her mother's pregnancy. Seemingly her father was not. On 25 September 1935, Jennifer Louise Lee was born.

They returned home to Amersham in Buckinghamshire and two and a half years later her sister was born. Their grandparents lived nearby, so the girls saw much of them. Jennifer was particularly close to her grandfather, to whom she devotes a whole chapter in *In the Midst of Life*.

The girls' early education took place just round the corner at Kingsley House School. This was a small private school run by a Miss Helliwell. As a young child, Jennifer was always fearless and very competitive. Her aim was to go further or climb higher than anyone else. This could well be how she managed to fall out of a tree in the playground, gashing her thigh severely on a stump beneath.

In 1945 the girls were sent to Belle Vue School. The school had been evacuated from London early in World War II, initially to Little Chalfont and later, in 1946, to Hyde End, near Great Missenden. The girls caught the steam train to school and later, when it moved to Hyde End, they caught the school bus from Amersham station in the winter months and cycled in the summer. The headmistress was one Miss Plummer and her deputy, Miss Cedargreen.

This was not a happy time for Jennifer – she showed not the slightest inclination towards academic study, and if ever rules were made to be broken, Jennifer was there to break them. Her school reports make very interesting reading. 'Jennifer's work would be good if she worked consistently.' 'Jennifer's work is spoilt completely through her lack of care and inability to work consistently.' 'Jennifer must remember "rules" must be obeyed.' 'Jennifer needs to learn more thoroughly. She must be more careful.'*

Seemingly, Jennifer's least favourite subject was mathematics, particularly algebra. It is quite likely that it was this lesson she decided to miss on one memorable occasion during the summer term. The grounds of Belle Vue School were very beautiful and a walk held much greater appeal than an hour of algebra. Everything went according to plan and Jennifer successfully made her escape. However, her plans took a dramatic and painful turn for the worse when she stepped in a wasps' nest! Angry wasps swarmed all over her, stinging her terribly from head to toe. Discovery was inevitable as everybody rushed outside on hearing the dreadful screams. The headmistress had to be summoned of course, and matron. Jennifer received first aid but little sympathy – after all, she was breaking the rules and '"rules" must be obeyed'. She was sent home for the rest of the day to recover, but was nonetheless expected to cycle.

Jennifer left Belle Vue as soon as she was able, at the end of the summer term of 1950, two months before her fifteenth birthday. She left school with a final report but no certificates. Presumably she didn't take any exams, because she most surely would have kept the certificates had she done so. 'Jennifer needs to make greater effort. She is far too inert and lax.' This was the final

* At this point it would be worth noting that all her life Jennifer kept things – letters, postcards, reports, certificates, documents and all manner of small items. Her school reports are the earliest of these. Little did she realise how valuable this collection would be in the years to come.

comment from the headmistress, with three conduct marks and two good marks – not a great start to the next stage of her life!

Undaunted, Jennifer enrolled on a Pitman's shorthand and typing course. She must have been quite good at this as she managed to secure a job at Dr Challoner's High School in Amersham, as secretary to the headmaster. The year was 1951. She was just sixteen years of age.

It was during this period that she fell deeply in love with an older, married man. Her relationship with him was to have a profound effect on her, lasting her entire life. It was a relationship they both knew could go nowhere, so she left her job and, with a broken heart, set off on her travels. She packed a rucksack and hitch-hiked around the country, taking odd jobs wherever she could. Very little is known about this period of her life, but she certainly spent some time waitressing in Blackpool. Whatever she got up to, she had time to think and to plan her future, and so it was that she returned from her travels and started her nurse's training at the Royal Berkshire Hospital, Reading. The year was 1954.

Jennifer had finally found her vocation. She fell into nursing naturally and quite brilliantly. Indeed, in 1956 she received first medical prize, presented to her by Group Captain Douglas Bader, CBE, DSO, DFC, no less! So much for 'Jennifer needs to make greater effort. She is far too inert and lax.' However, old habits die hard and she still struggled with '"rules" must be obeyed'. On one famous occasion she allowed two friends, Jimmy and Mike, to stay in the drying room of the nurses' home. They stayed for three months and were never discovered. Had they been, Jennifer would have been instantly dismissed. (A full account of this story can be found in *Call the Midwife*.)

In 1957, after three years of intensive training, Jennifer was awarded her certificate as a State Registered Nurse.

After the discipline and constraints of a nurse's training, Jennifer needed a break – she needed to spread her wings and fly a little. She also wanted to learn to speak French. A spell in Paris was the answer. She placed a short advert in *Le Figaro* stating that a 'British Trained Nurse, experienced with children' sought a job in Paris. Forty replies arrived, all in French. Not to worry. A gentleman friend who spoke French agreed to translate the letters, select the best, and compose a reply. The poor man was highly embarrassed when, in a restaurant where they had agreed to meet, Jennifer said, in clear ringing tones, 'When we've had our meal, I want you to look through all these French letters and pick out the best'!

And so it was that Jennifer came to be an au pair in Paris for a few short but very happy months. She explored the streets of the beautiful city, went to concerts and galleries, and made new friends, one of whom, Helga, became a lifelong friend. In total, she au paired for three families, mastering the French language all the while – so much so that she eventually felt confident enough to apply for a nursing job in a French hospital. She planned to stay for several months, but in the end left after just five days. She was witness to the harsh treatment of an unmarried pregnant girl, intended to teach the girl a lesson and to be an example to others. Jennifer promptly left and never went back. Her Paris days were over, and with some relief she returned to London where she began her training to be a midwife. Back in the fifties it took a year to train as a midwife. Training was taken in two parts and it was during Part 2 that Jennifer was sent to a nursing order of nuns in the East End of London.

What followed was the period of her life recounted so brilliantly by her own pen in *Call the Midwife*, *Shadows of the Workhouse* and *Farewell to the East End*, each one a masterpiece of writing. It was the start of a career that lasted twenty years. It was without a doubt the most formative period of her life; it opened her eyes to an entirely different world of traditions, cultures, attitudes and expectations. The experience also opened her heart and mind to a faith embodied by the nuns, which she carried with her for the rest of her life.

She completed her midwifery training in September 1959, shortly after her twenty-fourth birthday. What to do next? She toyed with the idea of becoming a missionary nurse at Lambaréné Hospital in what was known then as French Equatorial Africa (now Gabon). She went as far as applying for a job, and indeed was offered one by Dr Schweitzer, who had founded the hospital in 1913. However, by this stage in her life she had committed herself to God: she felt she could not leave the care of her church and so she turned the offer down.

Instead she took a series of jobs at various hospitals in and around London, including the London, the Elizabeth Garrett Anderson and the Marie Curie. Jennifer was ambitious, steadily climbing the career ladder, and by 1961 she was ward sister at the Queen Mary Maternity Home, near Hampstead. This was a specialised hospital caring purely for pregnant women with conditions dangerous to mother or child, or both.

One particular patient, Jackie, was admitted to the hospital early in September 1961, suffering from pre-eclampsia, a condition graphically recounted in *Call the Midwife*. She was confined to complete bed rest until her daughter's birth four weeks later. She and Jennifer formed a bond which developed over the weeks of Jackie's confinement. One afternoon, Jackie was describing her brother to a fellow patient – 'tall, good-looking, a brilliant brain and crazy about classical music'. Jennifer, who was writing up notes at the next bed, overheard. 'He sounds just like the man I'd like to marry.' And so it was that Jennifer met 'a certain young man' fleetingly referred to at the end of *Farewell to the East End*, and as they say, 'the rest is history'!

Suzannah Hart

That 'certain young man' was Philip Worth, Jackie's brother, something of a loner, who had escaped some years before from an overprotective family situation in Edinburgh to seek his fortune in London. This 'fortune' turned out to be a succession of poorly paid clerking jobs with various law firms, well below his intellectual abilities, and at the time they met he was deeply uncertain about his future and next career move.

His next move turned out to be a domestic one when he became Jennifer's lodger in her recently acquired home in Hampstead Garden Suburb. Predictably, this move was engineered by Jackie and had huge significance for both Jennifer and Philip. The physical proximity of living under the same roof no doubt contributed to their bonding, but more important (apart from physical attraction) was closeness of outlook on life generally and shared cultural and intellectual interests. From the start, there was a rapport between Jennifer and Philip. He was going through a difficult time, disappointed by his poor achievement since graduating in arts and law at university, and confused and uncertain about the way ahead. In Jennifer he found a ready and sympathetic listener to his problems and felt relaxed and at ease in her company as he talked about them. He also found himself falling in love.

One thing led to another, and Philip proposed marriage. Jennifer requested a week to think about it (mother was consulted) but to his utter delight she accepted and they were married at St Jude-on-the-Hill, Hampstead Garden Suburb, on 4 April 1963. They honeymooned in France, firstly in Paris, then in the Alpes-Maritimes, in a chalet owned by an Englishman who grew roses for sale in the Nice flower market and also cultivated a few vines. The wine that he made from these he distilled to produce a potent spirit he called Aqua Vitae, strong enough to burn a hole in sheet metal. Their host was a chess addict and would frequently visit in the evening armed with chess set and wine. Conscientious in his hospitality, he assured his guests that the twin beds in the chalet could easily be joined together to make a double, in discreet recognition of their newly married status.

Marriage brought major changes to the lives of both Jennifer and Philip. Philip entered teaching, a much more congenial profession for one with his academic background. Jennifer continued nursing on a part-time basis, but entered motherhood with the birth of two lovely daughters, Suzannah and Juliette, in 1964 and 1966, respectively.

The birth of their two daughters also meant a transfer of the family home from Hampstead to something larger, in Hemel Hempstead, Hertfordshire – firstly to a four-bed semi in Bennetts End and later to the White House in Boxmoor. Jennifer was an avid gardener and it was for this reason that they bought the White House. It had a huge rambling garden, sadly neglected, and over the years Jennifer transformed it into something truly wondrous.

Her part-time nursing helped to keep Jennifer's interest in medical matters alive, but she was becoming increasingly concerned by what she saw as the bureaucratisation of the National Health Service. In particular, she deplored the move towards putting management boards in charge of hospitals and abolishing the post of matron. In Jennifer's view, the matron occupied a unique position in the nursing hierarchy, a figure of great, often awesome, authority, but one whose priority was the care and welfare of her patients. She felt that the substitution of, and obsession with, professional management skills were not healthy developments, particularly as many of the so-called managers had scant, if any, direct experience of the medical world.

Jennifer's preoccupations were not confined to hands-on medical practice. She was a thinker, deeply sensitive to all aspects of the human dilemma but especially to social attitudes towards death and dying, which she regarded (quite reasonably) as natural and inevitable, to be faced frankly and realistically and not treated as taboo subjects, as is the modern tendency in the Western world. In the early 1970s she organised an important forum, chaired by the then bishop of St Albans and consisting of speakers from the NHS, from academia and from two sects of the Christian church, to discuss these issues publicly. The forum was well attended in a local school hall, and was in no way affected by a power cut necessitating the use of candles!

Eventually, thoroughly disillusioned by the direction in which the profession appeared to be heading, Jennifer retired from nursing in 1973.

Long before commencing her career as an author, Jennifer's great passion was music, a love she shared with Philip. Although he himself could neither sing nor play a musical instrument, he was greatly impressed by his wife's singing voice which could be heard all round the house as she went about her daily chores. Philip urged Jennifer to have her voice trained. She had a succession of teachers and over the years the quality of her singing went from strength to strength, enabling her to give solo performances in public and eventually gaining her a fellowship at the London College of Music. She learned to play the Gaelic harp and loved to accompany herself on this instrument, singing mainly Scottish and Irish folk songs. On one visit to the Edinburgh Festival she took her harp (and her voice) out onto the streets of the city and busked. This attracted much attention, not simply for her music but also because she was resplendent in tartan skirt and plaid – a nice bit of local colour, pleasing to the ear and to the eye!

Jennifer had learned to play the piano as a child, but her playing was somewhat neglected during her nursing career. She found a notable piano teacher, Jackie Chapling, who brought her back to the standard required to become a teacher herself. Jennifer taught piano and singing very successfully for over twenty years.

Another feature of musical life was the gatherings at the White House, which Jennifer and Philip organised, the highlight of which were performances by talented musicians culled from their network of friends and acquaintances. Always hugely popular occasions, guests would be entertained by pianists, violinists, singers, mime artists, etc., and on one memorable occasion by a one-man band with about six different instruments, including drums, cymbals and castanets, attached to various parts of his anatomy. Refreshments on offer were usually bread and cheese, wine and home-made beer (the latter withdrawn after some of the bottles exploded!).

Jennifer was always a firm believer in the motto 'a healthy mind in a healthy body'. She followed two main routes to physical fitness: swimming and cycling. For years the couple owned a flat in Brighton, a four-minute walk from the sea. This took care of the swimming.

Cycling had featured at different times in her life: as a schoolgirl, as a midwife in Poplar, and inspired by the activities of her daughter Suzannah and her son-in-law, Tim, both enthusiastic members of the local cycling club. Jennifer also hero-worshipped Bernard Hinault, five times winner of the Tour de France. In her mid-sixties Jennifer took up cycling once again. A suitable bicycle was required. Not for Jennifer an off-the-rack bike from Halfords. No indeed. At great expense and with help from Tim, she purchased a succession of handmade bikes, culminating in her own customised bicycle, with 'Call the Midwife' emblazoned on the frame. On these she explored the countryside for miles around, both solo and in groups, having many an adventure on the way. She frequently got lost and had numerous punctures, which she was ill equipped to repair. She often came home extremely late, causing Philip endless worry, but she always arrived safely, tired but happy, totally unaware of the worry she had caused.

And so we come to Jennifer's writing. Having spent twenty

years nursing and twenty-five years teaching music, she turned to a third career and, when she did, the reading public knew all about it! She had always been a storyteller, inventing bedtime stories, which she later wrote down. In her early sixties Jennifer suffered a period of acute eczema. She discovered a connection with food allergies and felt the need to write about it. A short book was privately published, which achieved modest success, but more to the point, she had discovered in herself a talent for writing.

Jennifer never saw herself as an author, but the challenge to do for midwives what James Herriot had done for vets was enough to trigger an explosion of literary energy which eventually culminated in the best-selling trilogy *Call the Midwife*, followed by the record-breaking BBC series of the same name. The success of her books took her somewhat by surprise, but she was delighted nonetheless. Letters started arriving through the post from people who had read and been captivated by her books and who felt compelled to write to tell her so. She kept each and every one of these letters and replied to them all. Her replies are now the treasured possessions of many of their recipients. When her agent contacted her to say the BBC was interested in turning her books into a series, she took it all in her stride and decided that she would go out for her bike ride as planned!

Philip Worth

Motherhood

Jennifer's huge success as a writer could not have been imagined all those years earlier when she was a hard-working mother of two. The house and income were very modest, the car was very old, and family holidays were never abroad. The family, plus two sickly Siamese cats, would pile into the old minivan, the two little girls balancing precariously on the wheel arches in the back. Jennifer was not one to worry over such trifles as road safety – indeed, on one famous occasion the back doors of the minivan flew open while they were travelling, nearly launching the girls into the road. Jennifer didn't fuss – she just shut the doors with a bang, secured the handles with a piece of string, and they continued on their way.

Their destination was usually Dorset, to stay in the little bungalow owned by Jennifer's mother. These holidays always featured long, healthy walks, hours on the beach in all weathers, and seemingly endless freezing swims in the sea. Jennifer was bold and adventurous and loved the sea, the choppier the better. She tried to toughen up her sensitive little daughters by taking them into the sea and was maybe a bit dismayed when they shivered and whined. However, if she was disappointed in anything her daughters ever did or said, she didn't show it.

Another frequent destination was Hastings, where Jennifer would take the girls to stay with the nuns who, by this time, had long since moved from the East End. There was a tiny caravan in the grounds of the convent and this is where they stayed. These holidays were very different from the bracing holidays spent in Dorset. They were quiet and genteel, but enjoyable nonetheless. Afternoon tea with the nuns and eating cinnamon toast was a particular treat. The girls developed a special fondness for Sister Jocelyn and a rich correspondence arose between them. Letters, cards and endless drawings were sent to and fro and, needless to say, Jennifer kept everything that Sister Jocelyn sent to the girls.

Growing up as Jennifer's daughters was incredibly enriching and rewarding. However, it was often challenging for two sensitive young girls with a desperate need to fit in. Jennifer's aspirations for herself and her family were never financial. What she constantly strived for was intellectual and creative endeavour. She also had a deep-rooted dislike of gossip and popular culture. The area where the family lived for more than ten years was Bennetts End, a typical new-town housing estate. While other mums wore 1970s flares and clumpy shoes, Jennifer wore handmade long velvet dresses and stilettos. While other families' houses were filled with TV and pop, the sound of Jennifer's singing practice emanated from the Worth family home. Much to the dismay of her daughters, Jennifer's scales and arpeggios could be heard halfway down the street.

Jennifer's daughters were often teased at primary school about their 'posh' mother, as the local kids described her. Being different certainly made life difficult for the girls, but the advantages far outweighed the disadvantages. Jennifer's complete disregard for school rules meant that often on sunny days she would take her daughters out of school and they'd all go cycling and picnicking by the canal. The fact that she also took her daughters swimming in those murky green waters is probably no surprise, but not a memory to be treasured.

Jennifer was always an outdoor type and wherever she went the girls went too. Apple-picking in her father's orchard was a memory of family endeavour that typically ended in near-disaster. Jennifer always wanted to go the furthest, climb the highest, be the strongest and the bravest – she was fearless and reckless and the apple trees were a challenge too strong to resist. While the girls looked on in admiration tinged with fear, she reached for the furthest apple, breaking the branch she was perched on, sending her crashing to the ground into a huge pile of stinging nettles. Poor Jennifer was accident-prone all her life, but this was purely a result of her fearless and indomitable personality.

Life in the Worth house was extremely busy as the girls' cultural and creative life developed. From a very young age they learned piano, guitar, recorder, violin, double bass and clarinet; they took part in music camps, composition classes, orchestras, choirs, chamber groups and jazz ensembles.

When the girls reached their teenage years all this training was put to good use – while their friends had Saturday jobs in Woolworths and Timothy White's, Jennifer encouraged her daughters to earn money by singing at weddings and teaching the recorder. Jennifer took her daughters to the ballet, to concerts, to the theatre and recitals. Her constant thirst for creative and cultural experiences infused the family and meant there was never a dull moment or idle hour. In fact, teenage rebellion never featured in the Worth family household because there was just no time for such nonsense.

Although a very loving and devoted mother, Jennifer was a firm believer that young people should have adventures, try new experiences, and become independent at an early age. Again, the excitement and adventure of the girls' upbringing was often tinged with anxiety. Jennifer was not the sort of mother to be challenged and so, with a certain reluctance, as young teenagers the girls learned how to canoe, and with trepidation they cycled unaccompanied over the Black Mountains in Wales. At sixteen and seventeen they did their first InterRail trip around Europe. Jennifer, much later in life, admitted that she was very worried for her daughters' safety and was hugely relieved when they phoned from Paris to say they'd arrived.

Throughout their lives, Jennifer's daughters received much love and encouragement. She was not judgemental, but must have despaired at the unwholesome alliances made with unsuitable men. Eventually, both girls met suitable young men, of whom Jennifer approved. Much of this approval was based on the fact that her sons-in-law could both do useful, practical jobs about the house and garden. Rarely would a family occasion pass by without one or both of them being required to drill a hole, put up shelves, change a light bulb, wield an axe, climb up ladders, prune the bushes or turn the compost!

Suzannah and Tim bought a bright modern flat in good condition in Hemel Hempstead. Juliette, on the other hand, bought a bomb-damaged terraced house in Handsworth, Birmingham.

True to character, Jennifer kept her doubts about this dubious purchase to herself. Nonetheless, she was always ready to assist with Juliette's Heath Robinson-style repairs.

Suzannah became pregnant and three months later so did Juliette. Jennifer was thrilled and her instincts as a midwife came flooding back. She was present throughout the labour and birth of her first granddaughter, remaining calm, practical and reassuring. Three months later, her grandson was born to Juliette, and one year after that her second granddaughter was born to Suzannah.

Juliette Walton

On being a Grandma

Jennifer took to her role as Grandma with typical enthusiasm and commitment. She avidly supported her granddaughters' musical activities, clapping and cheering in the front row of every concert.

> The last time Grandma saw us perform was at a concert in Tring. As we stepped out to the front I noticed she had disappeared. Midway through our duet there was a sharp crash and shattering of glass – it could only have been our Grandma. Despite her eccentricities and odd little habits (she did once call herself a funny old bugger), I am proud to call her my Grandma.
>
> Ellie

Her three grandchildren had many adventures with her and viewed her eccentricities with a mixture of bewilderment and delight. She would turn a seemingly mundane activity into an exciting challenge.

> My memories of Grandma will always be happy – pushing us in the wheelbarrow to the allotment, not caring what people thought; clambering into the pond to get the weeds out. At

her instruction we would put on our scruffiest clothes to chop logs, cut down bushes and annihilate the ivy, or we would put on our best clothes to go to the ballet and excitedly queue up in the interval for ice cream.

Lydia

Much as she loved her granddaughters, Dan was special because she had always wanted a grandson. In Dan she saw the potential to relive some of the adventures of her childhood and explore the great outdoors.

Every time I would visit there would be some crazy plan or adventure being formed. When I was twelve my Grandma had a brainwave – we should go on a cycling holiday together – I was mortified, it was so uncool and embarrassing. Also I wasn't sure if I was ready to meet all those new people and fend for myself. At first I made friends with the other kids my age and we avoided Grandma, but after a time I started making time for the two of us and we actually really got on.

Dan

Jennifer loved, supported and nurtured her family and had a huge positive influence on all of their lives. Although she was a natural loner, she valued her family very highly and took great pride as she watched her children and her grandchildren flower.

Juliette Walton

In the Midst of Life

Jennifer started writing her fourth book in 2006. It was a book she had given much thought to for over twenty years, and with the success of the trilogy assured she felt the time was right once again to put pen to paper.

In the trilogy the focus is mainly on the beginning of life; her fourth book looks at the end of life. It was a subject very close to Jennifer's heart, and one that she felt should be discussed openly and honestly and not kept closeted away. So absorbed was she in the writing of this book, and concerned for its success, that she failed to spot the signs of her own failing health. This may be the case, or it could be that she simply chose to ignore them. We will never know.

In March 2011, after weeks of backache and perhaps a month of increasing difficulty with swallowing, she was finally persuaded to go into hospital. She had spent a few days on her own at the flat in Brighton, and when Philip joined her for the weekend he was shocked to see how weakened she had become. He took her straight to the Brighton hospital, where she was admitted for tests.

On Wednesday, 16 March, Suzannah visited, not just to see her mother but to give comfort and support to Philip. It was during this visit that Jennifer broke the shattering news to them both that she had been diagnosed with cancer of the oesophagus, with secondaries in her bones. She had consented to have a stent inserted to open up the oesophagus, but refused surgery to remove the tumour. Her wish was to be taken home to be cared for by her family and to let nature take its course. Above all, she wished for a peaceful and dignified end.

On Wednesday, 30 March, she returned home to the White House in Boxmoor, to her bedroom overlooking the garden she had so lovingly created. Her family took the greatest care of her and nothing was too much trouble. Her daughters prepared endless tiny meals, most of which were left untouched. Her granddaughters bathed her, washed and set her hair. Philip was by her side constantly. She received an endless stream of visitors, and letters and cards flooded through the letterbox, all wishing her the very best.

Her strength and courage in facing her own death were phenomenal. In fact, it was that courageous approach that gave her family the strength to face the situation and accept it calmly.

In her own words, she said to Suzannah, 'Darling, I don't want you crying for me, I don't want you to grieve for me. Death is as much a part of life as birth. I have no fear of death and there is no need for you to fear death either.' For Jennifer, death was part of life's journey and she regarded it simply as the next stage in that journey, to be embarked upon without fear.

Gradually the cancer overtook her body and she became weaker and weaker. She no longer had the strength to receive visitors, but still appreciated having the letters and cards read out to her. Philip sat with her for hours, chatting, reading aloud or simply holding her hand.

She finally slipped away on 31 May. It was early evening; the sun was shining, the birds singing. The end could not have been more peaceful, just as she wished.

Her death left a huge hole in the lives of those closest to her. Letters and cards once again started flooding in, offering love, support and condolences – but, without exception, each one carried the same overwhelming sentiment, that she was a truly remarkable woman.

Suzannah Hart

Jennifer sitting on the roof garden of Mission House in Poplar in the late 1950s. Even while knitting in a nurse's uniform, she still managed to maintain her regal expression and demeanour.

From a letter Jennifer wrote to friends and family in advance of the publication of Call the Midwife. *Little did she imagine then the enormous success it would become!*

June 2002

I am writing to all my friends and relatives about *Call the Midwife*. It is a lovely book that I'm sure a lot of people will want to read. The *Sunday Express* are doing a big feature about it in their magazine section on 7 July, so you can find out more there. This is a very exciting time and I am nervous about all the publicity, but thrilled at the same time.

I hope you enjoy reading it as much as I did in the writing.

God bless, & best wishes,
Jennifer

✦

Dear Ms Worth,

It is over 50 years since I wrote my one and only 'fan letter' (to Roy Rogers!) and I now feel compelled to do it again to you. The reason is your enthralling *Send for the Midwife*. I could not put it down and returned over and over again to the photographs. What an enjoyable experience and so utterly absorbing.

Both my late husband and I were born in Poplar, and as he died unexpectedly last year my mind has more frequently revisited our courting days. And when I opened your book I was immediately back in my childhood. I could even smell the smoke of the occasional train at the bottom of our street.

I was born in 1937 at home on the corner of Morris Road and Rifle Street at the bottom of Chrisp Street (always pronounced Chris Street). My mother and her mother were also born in the house, as was my younger sister; we all lived together, grandparents, parents and we girls. My Nan and Mum ran our coffee shop on the premises until war damage and rationing closed it. In the mid-50s my parents reopened it as a wool shop. I lived there until I was married in 1957. I don't remember the name of the lady who 'came in' to my Mum when she went into labour even though she has mentioned it over the years, and now, at 95, she cannot hold a conversation.

In 1942 I started at Hay Currie School Infants, then went to Alton Street Juniors and then to Raine's Foundation Grammar in Arbour Square, Stepney, which still holds reunions.

I met my husband, Charlie, at St Michael's and All Angels Church in St Leonard's Road and we were married there. He was born in Spey Street, which was 'over the (railway foot-) bridge' to us. He attended St Paul's Way School, as had my Mum when it was still called Thomas Street School.

Your book came into my hands by wonderful coincidence. I attended a neighbour's funeral and his son-in-law came up from Glastonbury. He commented on having driven through the London traffic and said that he understood why his Mum had never wanted to move back to London. I asked where she was from and he asked if I had 'ever heard of Poplar'. I said 'Not Much' and he mentioned lots of streets which his Mum spoke of but having been born in Somerset he knew nothing about them. He told me of this marvellous book he had seen and bought for his Mum and lent it to me. She had been evacuated to Somerset and so had Charlie's family and she was also born in Spey Street.

When I started my own family here in Dagenham in 1964 my GP believed in first births in hospital (but not the local ones) and subsequent ones at home. So he sent me to Bancroft Road, Mile End for my first and, as was his normal procedure, booked the Salvation Army Nurses and Midwives for the next two at home. What lovely ladies they were, and, as the same midwife attended both times as well as going to my neighbours, their local antenatal clinics were more like a social club of friends. I remember they were based in Clapton or Hackney but their clinic here has long since closed. In spite of my first home delivery resulting in a post-partum haemorrhage resulting in a visit from the 'flying squad' from Rush Green I firmly support home births and local midwives. I feel sorry for current mums-to-be with their quick dash to the labour wards trailing their 'birth partners' followed by an almost immediate return home before she has hardly got her breath back. Much more relaxing to have stayed at home in the first place, though probably most inconvenient to the present-day medical profession.

I am now recommending your book to everyone whether of my generation or not. I was surprised when my 30-year-old daughter asked to read it as I thought it too out of date for the new mums of today but she said it was really good and she did enjoy it. She was moved by your account of the lady with the premature baby tucked in her clothes. I told her that when we were children our family raised their own chickens and I remember taking my turn to keep the weakest of the 'day-olds' down inside my liberty bodice while Mum and Nan prepared dinner.

I thank you most sincerely for giving me back my Poplar which had disappeared among the post-war development. This book is not a glimpse of the past, it is a visit.

Yours faithfully,
Mrs Norah Dear

Norah Dear adds:

My family still refer to an old childhood friend of mine – we were always close as my Nan had brought up his Mum together with mine – and although his family moved to Wiltshire when he was a teenager he insisted he was East End to the core and loved coming to stay and visit all the old places, changed though they are now. His one regret was that his Mum was in the 'lying in' home in East India Dock/Commercial Road in labour with him when all the mums were moved out hurriedly due to a bombing raid – and to his everlasting annoyance his Birth Certificate shows he was born in Newport Pagnell of all places! He passed away a couple of years ago having never been back there and still insisting he was a Poplar boy.

Caroline Slack first wrote to Jennifer Worth in 2008, suspecting that one of the most beloved characters in Call the Midwife – *Sister Julienne – might, in fact, have been her aunt. She received this reply from Jennifer:*

Dear Mrs Slack,

I was overjoyed to get your letter and to know that you are a relative of Sister Jocelyn, who is Sister Julienne in my books, and who was probably the most influential person in my life. She was a saint.

I would love to meet you and to hear more about Auntie Jocy. I attended her weekly during her last illness, and went to the funeral service at the convent in Birmingham . . . Sister Jocelyn was a serious artist, watercolours and a big pile of her pictures went to the family after the funeral. I took two pictures which I treasure and they are framed and hang in my bedroom to this day. [These pictures are also mentioned in the correspondence of Sister Jocelyn, see page 56–57.]

Caroline writes:

It was so exciting to get [the letter] as it confirmed that the Sister Julienne I had been reading about in *Call the Midwife* was my aunt Jocelyn. Jennifer sounds just as excited as I was!

She was a remarkable woman and for me and my cousins and brothers an extraordinary link with our much loved and respected aunt who had died 18 years before. Our aunt had always been there for us but about her friends and professional life we knew very little. Jennifer reveals this warmth and love for Sister Jocelyn, her friend, godmother and nursing colleague, in her letter.

This was the beginning of a long correspondence and friendship:

We were struck by Jennifer's dynamism and energy when she came to our house for lunch shortly after sending me this letter. She arrived in her cycling shorts with her bike and at the end of the afternoon set off home on an arduous 9-mile bicycle ride, putting us all to shame!

In May 2009, Caroline wrote to Jennifer after reading the last book in the trilogy:

Dear Jennifer,

The only sad thing about reading *Farewell to the East End* is that I've come to the end and there are no more of your wonderful stories to read. I thoroughly enjoyed the last book that you so kindly sent me. I hope you didn't think me very rude for not thanking you sooner but I wanted to read the book first.

You have such a talent for all the details that transport one to the scene so easily – the crunch and the crackle, the whiffs and the wafts – and with such warmth and tenderness. And of course for me it is so personal. Sister Julienne or Jocelyn was *so* much a part of my childhood and adulthood. She was 'ours' but of course I realize now that she was so much more. Learning of the love and respect she earned in her professional life has been quite sobering. Families take themselves so much for granted. But I think she needed us too. Remarkable that she could have handled all the different demands on her life: the monastic discipline, the midwifery and the ups and downs in the lives of her mother, her five brothers, three sisters and all their children. We owe you a great debt for the books you have written about the dedicated and hard-working and courageous nursing nuns. So often when I mention nuns I get treated to stories of the abuse meted out by cruel school teachers, etc. in convents. You have done them a great service.

Caroline

✦

14 November 2009

Dear Jennifer,

I am writing to tell you how much I have enjoyed your books – *Call the Midwife* and *Farewell to the East End*. The first I found to be enchanting and amusing and the second, with its accounts of living conditions in the East End of the time reminds me of visits to both sets of grandparents in my childhood.

My first vivid memory of the East End was in 1944 – I suppose we hadn't been to London before that because of the war. I was six. We travelled by train from Slough where my father had bought a house out of London when war started. I remember the trams and the bomb damage and arriving at my grandparents' home in Pole Street, Stepney. The houses further up the road had been bombed but they luckily escaped. My grandfather had had a coal delivery business and my mother, the youngest of nine children, spoke of going with him on a horse and cart to deliver the coal. The house was small with a privy in the garden and I remember the horsehair pricking the backs of my legs while sitting on the sofa when banished to the parlour while the grown-ups talked. Looking back they were obviously so much better off than most.

On the other hand, when we left there and went to visit Dad's parents in Limehouse they were living in a council flat in an enormous block with outside stairs. Inside just two rooms and a small kitchen and bathroom. They had been bombed out and it was obviously not where they had been when they had their seventeen children. My father was third from the end. I never knew how many were left after the bombing – direct hits on the air raid shelter, killed in the army in the First World War, meningitis and no doubt other terrible traumas. Those

I met were dockers and doctors. My cousin Rosalind became a Dame for her services to Medicine and the Law and was at Queen Charlotte's Hospital in London. Two others, both men – one is Professor Emeritus at Yale University and his brother, sadly died, a Consultant in hospital in London, Canada, whose special care was the indigenous American Indians.

As you can imagine, with such an enormous family I haven't met them all, but I was amazed to see on television at the time of the dockers' strikes when the docks were closing, a young, burly man named Cornelius Clancy (my maiden name) and a cousin, leading the dockers and spokesman at the closed gates of the docks!

My own father as a boy sang in the choir at St Augustine's Church and, as a teenager alone on his bike, cycled as far as Norfolk. When my mother died and we took him to Norfolk on holiday he could still find the road and house where he took B&B! He trained as a tailor at a factory, Pollikoff's in Hackney, and became in middle life their Production Manager. After the war and his time in the Army, he travelled with a delegation to America studying new methods and machinery in the tailoring business. We lived in a modest terraced house just by the railway station where he caught the Workman's train to London every morning and I would run up the avenue to meet him at 7.15 every evening. He died aged 96.

For my elder sister and I education was a premium – my sister was an excellent pianist and accountant and I loved to sing (and still do). I became a secretary in the close by ICI Paints Division where I met my husband David, a Scot, whose father was a miner in Fife. Later, when the children were all at school, I worked as a secretary for a doctors' practice and became their Practice Manager until I retired. David and I, like you, married in the sixties, 1960 to be exact, and are coming up to our 50th anniversary. We have four lovely daughters and fifteen grandchildren, all clever and musical, playing a variety of instruments – piano, flute, clarinet, bagpipes, violin and classical guitar!

I have rambled on having just put down your book *Farewell to the East End*. The memories conjured up on reflection of your story have overwhelmed me and I will give the books to my daughters as a background to their ancestry. Also, when I think about it, give to them a copy of this letter as the story of my life! Thank you so much for your wonderful writing.

Yours sincerely,
Maureen Lessels

PS: My husband has also written a book, *A Tramp in Africa*, published by Pen Press, telling of a journey he made in Africa in the fifties. The story tells of the trek from Scotland to Cape Town, South Africa, living with the Africans in their villages and learning their language, wearing the kilt and being given lifts and taken into people's homes, and the incredible experiences and adventures he had.

Jennifer greatly enjoyed these memories:

Your experiences with the East End are fascinating. Your family with 17 children – dockers to Dames, one could say! Your husband's account of walking the length of Europe and Africa sounds quite astonishing. Both my husband and I would like to read it.

Dear Mrs Worth,

I am 52 years old and find myself writing to an author for the first time in my life. I just had to say thank you for two wonderful books.

Browsing through the bookshelves of a local shop for something to read on holiday, my eyes were drawn to *Shadows of the Workhouse*. Once on holiday I was transfixed from page one. I am a 6 foot tall, 14 stone biker trained in martial arts, but I am not ashamed to admit you made me weep with sadness more than once. As soon as I returned to the UK, I purchased *Call the Midwife*, which I read with equal pleasure, I just could not put it down. My wife has also read both books, she could not put them down either, it was great to get some peace and quiet . . . ha ha.

These books and your amazing life are now recorded for future generations to marvel at. The conditions you describe seem like something you would expect from a Dickensian novel, I can't believe they still existed when I was born in 1957. Even though the conditions were tough, I can't help thinking that society has lost something intangible that runs through every page of your story.

Please, if you still have stories untold, write another book, it will sell like hot cakes.

With much gratitude and thanks,
Paul Jennings

✦

Mary Williamson is the widow of Father Joe Williamson, the inspirational minister Jennifer recalls in Call the Midwife, *in particular for his work establishing a safe haven for the prostitutes of Cable Street and the surrounding area. He is mentioned by Jennifer in the dedication to* Call the Midwife *and was born in Poplar.*

28 September 2002

Dear Jennifer,

I wanted to write and tell you how very much I enjoyed *Call the Midwife* – I couldn't put it down! I am sending copies to two of my nieces, one of whom is a midwife, the other involved with a special care baby unit in Devon.

Not long before we were married Joe took me to Wellclose Square and Dock Street and also showed me the little church in Poplar where he was with the choir as a child – and the street where he was born and the Limehouse Cut, etc. I also went to Daphne Jones's Jubilee service at All Saints', Poplar. Of course, by then, so very much had changed – especially Cable Street!

I look forward to the sequel.

Yours sincerely,
Mary Williamson

The correspondence between Jennifer and Mary continued:

15 June

Dear Jennifer,

I read *Shadows of the Workhouse* with great interest – as in the case of *Call the Midwife* I just couldn't put it down once I'd started. It's 'a sad book' as one of my friends (who had read *Call the Midwife*) to whom I gave a copy, said. She was a nurse and worked in Manchester and Liverpool as well as knowing the East End.

The final story of the old soldier particularly struck a chord with me because it reminded me of an old lady in Birkenhead in the mid-70s. My rector came to me one day and said, 'Mary, I have a job for you. I do hope you will take it on. To tell you the truth I don't know who else I could ask to do it.' He'd been the day before to visit an old lady in a council bungalow on an estate which was part of his parish. He'd had difficulty in being admitted because she wouldn't open to anyone, least of all the social services. When he got inside he said he couldn't sit down because everything was so dirty and he was in his cassock and had a service to take later.

Anyway I said I would try. I was teaching full-time so I went the next Friday and at once saw what he meant. The smell was very strong. Poor old Daisy was incontinent – and, I discovered, paranoid. She had a little black cat which she'd had for at least 2 years since it was a kitten. It was *never* allowed out – so you can imagine the result. The kitchen was filthy and so was the bathroom and indeed the bed/sitting room. Beside the bed was a little table with a paraffin lamp with no lamp glass! – and she had an open fire next to that.

I talked to her and introduced myself and said I'd come again and she asked me to get her pension for her as the neighbours who usually got it were away – to cut a long story short I visited Daisy regularly once or twice a week after school and at the weekend, I got a key made so that I could get in. She wanted to make me a cup of tea – but I said I would do it. I went into the kitchen and scrubbed out 2 cups with Vim – and a teapot. I couldn't have drunk out of them as they were – but, like you, I realised how important it was to accept her hospitality. We would sit by the fire and recite poems we'd both learnt at school, *The Inchcape Rock* and so on. She was a darling. Eventually I bought some flannelette sheets and a new mattress with a plastic cover. I threw out the old sodden one and I made sure I washed her sheets at least once a week, often more. She said a woman she used to know called Mrs Brennan, lived up in the loft and poured water on her bed to spite her! I went up into the loft and told her there was no one there but it made no difference.

As soon as I got home from my visits I used to strip off and put everything in the washing machine – the smell was so persistent – *but* as Father Joe always said, when you really care your senses go out of the window and you forget the smell.

Daisy eventually had to go to hospital. While I was away in Essex on holiday, and the vicar was also on holiday, she spilt a pan of boiling water over herself. I don't know who found her or how she let people know (for I was her only visitor) but the lay-reader who was taking the service on the Sunday I got back told me. Daisy was adjudged not fit to live alone. They were very kind to her at the hospital in Chester. She no longer remembered my name but knew me as 'my friend'.

The rector and I became Trustees and got a Power of Attorney. I cleaned out her bungalow – I was determined not to leave it to the council workmen because I knew Daisy hid things in all sorts of nooks and crannies. In the end I found some £300 in English and Canadian notes (her sister was in Canada), which I banked. The cat went to a cat's home but had to be put down because it was past house-training.

In the large hospital ward where Daisy was there was an old lady called Annie. She was very thin – but even looked quite 'chic' in a shapeless hospital dress – as thin people can. She would wander up and ask for a fag. As I didn't smoke I got into the way of taking some sweets with me and she liked that. The staff told me Annie had been there for years – must have been 50 years, I should think. She had been put into the asylum because she had an illegitimate child!! That had been her home ever since.

Daisy died in 1975 and I sent her money (about £800 in all with what she had in the PO) to her sister in Canada – but she died before it reached her and it went to her husband's family, as he died too!

In 1976, Joe and I were married and a year later I left Birkenhead.

What a long letter! But there were so many similarities.

I found the ending to Sister Monica's story very moving.

I look forward to the third book.

Love,
Mary Williamson

✦

Dear Jennifer,

I hope you don't mind my writing. I have found your book *Call the Midwife* absolutely fascinating. We knew Father Joe from the early 1960s and through him became attached to the East End.

You have brought so much back to us – Poplar, Stepney, Isle of Dogs, Wapping, Shadwell. We still get there at least once a year but of course it has all changed.

'Father Joe' was a great friend for forty years. Also Daphne Jones (Were you in the Sisters of St John?) Nora Neale, Frank Rust, Olive Wagstaff, Angela Butler . . . All these and so many more (including several of the girls from Church House) have been and in some cases still are a part of our extended family.

You have such a wonderful way with words. We look forward to your next book.

Thank you again, sincerely,
Philip Mason

Philip Mason comments:

'Father Joe always said that his ordination was a miracle. Born in Poplar in 1895, his father was killed two years later whilst working in the East India dock. His mother was left with just four pence in the world and eight children to bring up single-handed. Young Joe had a fine singing voice so he joined the choir at St Saviour's church and loved it. It was during an early morning service that he knew God wanted him to become a priest, but it seemed out of the question because at that time priests came from a different class. He soon learnt that with God nothing is impossible and the miracle did happen for he was ordained by the Bishop of London in 1925.

Unlike Father Joe, Daphne Jones was born in the Cotswolds where her father managed the family estate. As a teenager Daphne had a strong sense of vocation which led her to train as a nurse at St Thomas's hospital, London. One day she joined a party of people from her church for a visit to East London. She had never been to Poplar before but as soon as she got off the bus she knew immediately that this was where she wanted to be.'

Daphne Jones was a parish worker at All Saints', Poplar, for 55 years and she worked alongside Father Joe Williamson in his refuge. She is mentioned in connection with Jennifer's story about the young girl Mary in Call the Midwife *and the book is partly dedicated to her.*

Dear Jennifer Worth,

I hope you do not mind me writing to you, but I am now reading your third book about your work/life in the East End and feel I need to write you.

The reason is that my father worked with 'Daffs' for many years, so when I saw that you had dedicated your first book to Daphne Jones it was a bit of a shock.

My father, Bill Flory, worked as bursar for All Saints' with Father Arthur Royal and many of the curates. He used to take many children on holiday to Five Oak Green with Father John Baggley. He also worked with the children that played on the bomb site/adventure playgrounds. His office was on the ground floor at Montague House above 'Daffs'' basement flat. I used to have my lunch in her flat when I was at George Green School, which was a very sparse home as she would give everything away!

Many a time I would wake up at home and find a small child sleeping in my parents' bedroom brought back by my dad. This was because something had happened to their mum and my dad and 'Daffs' didn't want them to go into 'care'. The smell of nit lotion still haunts me!

He had many a story to tell so how I wish he had written a book like you. I only have memories now, which your books bring back. My dad would have loved reading your books, but sadly he died many years ago, so it's lovely to read about the people he worked with.

For some reason your photo resembles Daphne in my memory, but memories can play tricks.

Anyway, thank you for reading this.

Regards,
Jill Hunt (née Flory)

Jennifer recalled 'Daffs' with great fondness, writing:

We share many things. Of course Daphne Jones had to be in the book – she was a saint and the daughter of very well-to-do people. She was also a friend of Mr Collett, who comes into the second book. She worked with Fr Joe Williamson when I knew Mary. I also knew Fr Royal, but I didn't know your father. All Saints' has a special place in my memory.

Jill Hunt also shares this memory of her father's time in the East End:

My father, Bill Flory, and Father John Baggley would take a group of children to a large house in Five Oak Green for holidays – it must have been owned by the Church. They would take all these 'streetwise' children and teenagers out for walks at night – remember that they were from London and had never been anywhere without street lighting – and they were absolutely terrified, the dark was completely black! Bill and John would play spooky tricks and make noises in the dark, leaving the 'hard' kids shaking in their shoes. The other trick they would play was to take them for a nice long walk in the woods. Streetwise children are not aware of boggy areas that just look like grass, so John and Bill would run off, skirting a lovely boggy area then call the children. They would run straight through into the mud, much to the amusement of my dad and John!

Dear Mrs Worth,

I have just read your book *Shadows of the Workhouse* with great interest, and I felt that I had to write to you about it in some detail.

Please forgive me for taking such a liberty but I hope that the enclosed notes may excuse my action and perhaps be of some interest to you.

I am 87 and my mother and father were both born in Stoke-on-Trent. Leaving school at about 13 years of age my father went to work underground at Chatterley-Whitfield colliery, and my mother worked in a 'pot-bank'.

She never liked the work and she got a crazy idea that she would like to become a nurse, so she enrolled in a course of hospital nursing at the local 'workhouse'. She duly qualified, married my father early in World War I, after which he went into the army and she then qualified as a midwife and took herself off to industrial Lancashire as a Health Visitor.

After the war they both returned to the Potteries, she went back to the infirmary and he resumed his job as a miner. Before long, however, he left the pit and got a job as porter in the 'workhouse' where my mother was a nurse in the infirmary.

They later moved to the workhouse in Oxford (where I was born in the Radcliffe Infirmary) and at the end of 1922 they took up the joint appointment as Master and Matron of the workhouse at Oswestry in Shropshire.

Being brought up in that establishment from the end of 1922 until 1940 gave me a unique insight into the working of the old workhouse system, the very real fear of the workhouse by people suffering from the effects of the Depression, and the gradual changes in the care of the aged and infirm brought about by the introduction of the Public Assistance system.

Because of this I was particularly interested in your book. I remember the days when families were split up on admission to what you rightly describe as a 'place of last resort' and I recall the numbers of illegitimate children in the nursery. Interior walls were painted, the lower parts dark brown and the upper parts a rather depressing shade of dark green known to the trade as 'Workhouse Green'. The whole place was inadequately lit by gas and in the early part of 1923 it still had many characteristics of a Dickensian workhouse.

Apart from trying to brighten up the house and improve the general living conditions my parents were very much concerned about the aimlessness of life for the inmates and the lack of anything to interest them and to keep their minds active.

Local people were encouraged to form concert parties and to visit the institution at regular intervals, particularly during the winter months. These entertainments played an important part in the lives of the inmates because anticipating a concert gave them something to which they could look forward, the evening of the event provided a talking point (and sometimes the opportunity for a 'sing song'), and then the promise of another concert within a week or so gave them something to think about and to anticipate.

The staff also staged entertainments, especially on the evening of Christmas Day. According to photographs in my possession both my parents had featured in similar concerts in workhouses in Stoke-on-Trent and Oxford, and they continued the practice at Oswestry. In 1928 the staff produced a Pierrot show for the entertainment of the inmates and I still have a photograph of that group showing me – aged 6 – in Pierrot costume seated in the centre of the front row with a drum!

Many of the inmates in the early 1920s were mentally or physically handicapped. The majority were unable to read or write, but there were some notable exceptions. One was a FRCO whose wife had died and one of whose sons had been killed in the Great War of 1914–18. When his only surviving son had quarrelled with him, left home to get married and then vanished from his father's life, the gentleman suffered a severe mental breakdown and became 'institutionalised'.

Then there was Jimmy. He was a truly remarkable man. Not only could he read, but he could write in an immaculate 'copper-plate' hand, was quite a talented amateur artist – and could even play the piano. Because of his ability he was employed in helping my father in the 'workhouse' office, and was even allowed to play the piano in our private living room. Because Mum and Dad (living over the shop) were on call 24 hours a day, they had little time to spend with me and Jimmy became almost a second father to me. He taught me to read and write before I went to school, took me for walks in the countryside, made me books of his own drawings and taught me old music-hall songs. Apparently he had once been in the Guards, and he told me stories about his exploits in the Boer War, and stories about ghosts he had encountered while on sentry duty in the Tower of London.

He died about 1930 and I have always regretted that I never knew more details about his early life and how he came to end up in the workhouse.

I also remember the tramps who used our casual wards on a regular basis. They were a mixed bunch. Some of them were youngish men honestly looking for work during the Depression, some were alcoholics, some were from broken homes, some were criminals released from gaol, some were petty criminals on the run from the police, and some were what we would now call 'drop-outs'. I remember one who had obviously seen better days. Several times my father tried to persuade him to come into the house on a permanent basis, but he always refused.

'When I first went on the road,' he said, 'I hated it. I felt degraded. But now I quite like it. I'm my own boss, I don't owe anybody anything, and I go where I like when I like. I see the country and I see the town. I see the changing seasons; and when I die somebody will bury me.'

Contrary to popular belief tramps were not all dirty, verminous individuals – because those who used casual wards on a regular basis often had as many as 2, 3 (or even 4) baths a week! They didn't all like having baths and I remember one man who insisted that 'the doctor' had told him not to have a bath. When questioned he was unable to give any details as to why 'the doctor' had issued those instructions and the officers were suspicious. They ordered him to strip and he was then found to have a wide bandage right round his waist.

'That's why I haven't got to have a bath,' he said. 'The doctor told me not to get that bandage wet.'

Further questions failed to produce any satisfactory explanation and the officers finally put him in the bath of hot water. Almost immediately the water turned brown – and then it was found that he had packets of tea and sugar hidden in the bandage!

By the time I went to Oswestry the jobs of oakum-picking and stone-breaking for casuals had been abandoned, but the stone-breaking cells still existed. They were small single rooms not much larger than a toilet cubicle, lit by a metal grille in the outside wall, and the work of the tramps was to break stones until they could be pushed through the holes in the grille.

There were also women among the tramps, usually accompanying men to whom they may – or may not – have been married, but many moved around alone. One of these was a regular visitor known as 'Methylated Martha'. She was usually brought in by the police who had found her under a hedge, and she used to tell me that, no matter how cold the weather or how heavy a frost, she could sleep under a hedge and never feel the cold if she could wrap herself in a newspaper and have a drink of methylated spirits.

With this background you will understand why I found your book particularly interesting. I can relate, to some extent, to many of the things you describe; but on the other hand I recall other events form the mid-1920s and the 1930s which were rather more uncommon. For instance, I remember the coming of the wireless, when speakers were installed in the dining hall and the dayrooms, and every bed in the infirmary was equipped with headphones. None of the inmates had ever heard a wireless, and they had no idea of what it was all about.

Dad went round to all the patients in the infirmary and fitted headphones on them to see if they fitted comfortably. He placed them over the ears of one old lady and said to her 'Now, Mary, what do you think of that?' She gazed at him for a moment or two, then she shook her head and said, 'I'm sorry, Master, but I can't see any better now!'

Then there were the occasions in the mid-1930s when the staff raised funds by organizing whist drives and took all those inmates who were fit to travel (and the children from the nursery) for a day trip to Rhyl. Those were indeed memorable days when the inmates enjoyed lunch and tea in a proper restaurant and served by waitresses in uniform – something way beyond their normal experience.

The first of these trips was particularly memorable to me because I discovered that all the inmates who went to Rhyl spent some of their small hoard of coppers in buying souvenirs of the trip to give to those inmates who, for one reason or another, were unable to make the trip!

To refer again to your book, I noted your comments in the Epilogue about photographs. I have a number of photographs of the inmates taken on the trips to Rhyl, some of children in the nursery near a decorated Christmas tree, some of the children enjoying the sunshine in one of the outdoor areas, some women and children with me in one of the yards, an inmate who was the workhouse baker photographed carrying a tray of loaves outside the bakehouse, and patients in the infirmary wards.

Throughout my childhood in the workhouse I was encouraged to play with the children in the nursery, associate with all the inmates and take part in all their activities. Above all I was taught by my parents to treat them all with respect; and my upbringing in these circumstances has, I like to think, shaped my character and given me standards which have stayed with me throughout my life.

For that I am eternally grateful.

With all good wishes,
Yours sincerely,
Syd Bailey

In her reply to Syd Bailey, Jennifer wrote:

Thank you so much for writing and for sending me all your recollections of workhouse life from the inside in the 1920s and 30s. Your parents were obviously a very enlightened Master and Mistress, and life for the inmates depended entirely on the character of individual Masters. What you say about entertainment is very different from what I heard about Poplar workhouse, which was one of the worst in London, I'm told. The House at Liverpool was even more terrible. Built for 3,000, it often housed 5,000!! Your story of the organist (FRCO) shows that *no one* could say they would not end up in the workhouse – it is a very sad story.

✦

Jennifer first met Robert Runcie in the early 1970s when he was Bishop of St. Albans. She wrote to him, inviting him to take part in a medical forum she was organising. He replied, offering to be chairman of the event. He was Bishop of St. Albans until 1980 and during all that time she remained in close contact with him.

She took Suzannah and Juliette to visit him at the Abbey, where he would frequently greet them in full bishop's regalia. Much to the girls' delight he let them try on his bishop's ring and hide underneath the folds of his cloak. Jennifer took them to tea at the bishop's house where he showed them his pigs (a special interest of his), which were kept in the garden. He instructed the girls how to tickle a pig behind the ears with a stick, assuring them it was what pigs like best.

The contact continued by letter during the 1980s when he became Archbishop of Canterbury and during the 1990s when he retired. He was a great support to her and was always ready to offer advice and guidance when needed.

26 November 1997

Dear Jennifer,

Thank you very much for your thoughts about me and my health. It is true that my radiotherapy did me some good and I am leading a very active life indeed.

We have been away to Syria and the Lebanon. I was lecturing on a cruise. Since then we have been in California and I was giving a number of talks around San Francisco and San Diego. Since I have only just returned I hope you will forgive a brief reply. I am glad to have all the details about the conference and your splendid paper. I agree with you that the speakers seem somewhat unbalanced and there ought to be somebody from world religions and from the hospice movement. I don't have time to construct a quotable statement about the modern attitude to death. Long ago Bishop Anthony said, 'If we knew how to live we would know how to die; and if we knew how to die we would know how to live.' You might care to use that. It says a great deal in a nutshell about the revolutionary attitude which sees life as giving rather than taking.

If you do want to get names of people who can speak for Islam and Hindu communities I cannot do better than recommend you to get in touch with a man called Mr Brian Pearce, 5–7 Tavistock Place, London WC1H 9SS. He is Director of the Inter-faith Network. He is an admirable and well-informed character. If you mention my name I am sure he will put you onto the right people.

I hope all goes well and will think of you at the conference.

Yours ever,
The Rt Revd Lord Runcie

✦

In 1953, Coronation Year, I was a pupil midwife in Poplar, east London, with the Sisters of St John the Divine, as portrayed in the recent TV series *Call the Midwife*.

We were three pupils, and we were there for six months, having already spent six months at a maternity hospital. I had been at the British Hospital for Mothers and Babies at Woolwich, on the other side of the River.

The East Enders were mostly not well off but surviving. Because I spoke with a Coventry accent rather than Cockney they thought I was a 'toff'!

At the convent there was a very elderly Sister who could remember when the people were really very poor (early in the twentieth century), and she said the Sisters tried hard to get the mothers a square meal before they had their babies.

Everywhere was black with soot from all the chimneys of the houses, and also the boats on the river. I remember coming back to Warwickshire for a weekend and being surprised to see the trees were brown.

The previous year, when I was at Woolwich we had the Great Smog and many people died from chest conditions or even by falling into the river. The fog swirled about even inside the hospital, and the little premature babies in the nursery had black 'moustaches'!

One incident in the film did not ring true – when one of the nurses said she would like to go to look after black babies in Africa, the Sister replied that there were plenty of black babies here. In fact, a) there were not many at that time, and b) the Sisters did encourage us to go to Africa. One had been there herself, and two or three of us did go to work in what was then Tanganyika, with a missionary society.

Life was not quite as dramatic as the film showed although we had our moments! I was never so glad in my life as when the ambulance men raced up the stairs with the drip *already running* for my patient who was in serious trouble.

A few years previously, in 1947, after the war, the men came back from the Services, and the birth rate doubled!

One of the pupils at that time was Daphne Hoey-Jones, and as she was working nearby, she would sometimes drop in and tell us of those hectic days. She went on to work as a social worker in the East End and in fact did so all her life, and there is now a picture of her and some other saints of that part of London in All Saints' Church, which I visited again a few years ago. (Her story would make a film itself!)

Life was interesting and we had quite a lot of fun too, in spite of the fact that it rained a lot that year, I am sure the Queen remembers it.

We were extremely busy and there was absolutely no time for romance (!!) whatever the film showed.

Dear Jennifer Worth,

I don't know if you will receive this letter, but I hope you will. I have just read and really enjoyed *Shadows of the Workhouse*. Therefore I was interested to read another of your books, so sent off for *Call the Midwife*. This area you write about is of great interest to me as I was born in 1944 in Hackney, opposite Victoria Park, and then lived in Bethnal Green from 1952 to 1956. As my father was a congregational minister in Bethnal Green, we lived a slightly separate life. We moved to the flat over the congregational church, after it was repaired, as it had bomb damage from the war. My father was Rev. William Simpson, he also worked a lot in Poplar. He then became Moderator of London and we moved to Blackheath.

The reason for this letter is the picture on the front of *Call the Midwife*. I am convinced the little girl on the left is either me or my twin sister Ruth, and possibly the next little girls Sandra Silk and Janet Silk. There were five of us in our family, Ruth and I being the youngest. We have many happy memories of growing up in the East End of London. Each year my father took young people on camping holidays in the country, so each summer we spent weeks in old army tents enjoying the fields, fresh air and wonderful times with other young people from that area.

Would love to know who the children are in the photo.

As you can guess we have retired to a very rural area of France, we have been here for a couple of years. I love living in the countryside. I am most fortunate.

Regards,
Ann Croft

19 January 2010

Dear Mrs Worth,

I hope you won't mind my writing to you but I have found *Farewell to the East End* particularly fascinating because about one hundred years earlier, my grandmother's father, Henry Gaster (1835–1896), a chemist, worked in exactly the same area as you did. His death certificate describes him as *accoucheur*.

He was born at 39 Cotton Street, baptised and married at All Saints' Church, Poplar. His first shop, 1860, was in Robin Hood Lane and his family lived at 29 Kerbey Street by 1871 and an address later in his life was 159 Grundy Street. Henry's father Thomas Gaster lived at 26 Woodstock Road and he was Surveyor of Shipping to Trinity House. Ancestors were shipwrights in Stepney and my branch of the family produced many clergy, medical missionaries and teachers. Henry's brother Edwin Gaster occupied premises at Trinity Ballast Offices, Narrow Street.

My grandmother, the youngest of Henry's family, never went out to work and she used to deliver prescriptions to patients, many of whom could not pay. Evidently she went about safely. She was married at 20 to Arthur Gosling, FRCO, from Dorset and eventually, before his early death at age 39, they lived on the Hampstead Garden Suburb.

Regrettably when I lived in Ealing (where a Vicar had been at All Saints', Poplar, in the 1930s) I never visited the docks area. I have a reproduction of John Bratby's Isle of Dogs painting *Just Before They Took the Lighters Away*. I must obtain Professor Fishman's books.

Henry Gaster would have seen the establishment of the Convent in 1878.

My GP in Yorkshire, Ronald Plested and his wife Mary, a

physiotherapist, both trained at the London. About contemporary with you and me age-wise probably.

Thank you for the impressive record which your book gives of the work of midwives in social conditions which at times sound as grim as they would have been in great-grandfather's time.

Yours sincerely,
Lorna Knight (née Gosling)

✦

Dear Jennifer Worth,

I just had to write to say how much I enjoyed your book. It brought back many memories to me, as I knew the area reasonably well, having lived most of my childhood in Bishopsgate police station from the age of three to eighteen years. My father was a City copper, and we lived in the flats provided for families of the police which were situated behind the front entrance of the station in Bishopsgate. I went to school at Central Foundation Girls' School in Spital Square, finishing up at Sir John Cass in Aldgate, where I learnt shorthand typing and office work. It was recommended that I go to an art school, but my parents thought it didn't offer me a financial future, so I was persuaded to take up typing.

My father and mother came from the East End. Mum worked in London Hospital for a few months, and was a school secretary just off Whitechapel Road in a Jewish school. She said it was a very happy time of her life. Sadly she passed away five years ago at the age of ninety. I'm seventy-two next week, and left school in 1951. I had a school friend who lived down Cable Street. It was a joke in the school, keep away from Cable Street or you will get a knife in your back!

I have gone on far too long, especially as this letter was to say how much I enjoyed your book and can't wait to read your next one. I do have a problem with the sadness in the book, which brings back memories of my mother's comments about her and her mother's fear of the workhouse and her not being able to go to school some days because they had to share the shoes between six of them. It was always a fear she had, and hard for my sister and me to understand. Discussions about old people's homes were taboo. Another story!

Once again, thank you for writing such an interesting book and for all the enjoyment I got from it.

Yours sincerely,
Julie Gale

✦

Dear Mrs Worth,

I have just finished reading the first two books of your Nonnatus House trilogy and I await the third with great impatience. My cousin Caroline Slack sent me the first book, saying that it featured our Auntie Jocey. She didn't tell me which particular Sister in the book she was, but there were various pointers that made Sister Julienne the most likely candidate, and when I reached page 133 of the paperback edition I found the definitive clue which clinched the matter: 'Sister Julienne's eyes twinkled.' I am so excited and so grateful that you have painted such a consistently true portrait of my dearly beloved and much missed aunt.

The books have made a huge impression on me and the many cousins who have now read at least the first of the two. When I told my friend the vicar of St Mary's, Cable Street, that he must read *Call the Midwife*, he said he'd already read it, and that it was the best account of life in Docklands that he knew of. These books have opened my eyes to the true nature of Auntie Jocey's work. I had absolutely no idea that she worked under such conditions. She kept that side of her life mostly hidden from her family (partly out of discretion but also, I suppose, because she thought we wouldn't be interested), and her calm, good-humoured, ever-optimistic demeanour betrayed nothing of what she must have experienced as some truly appalling and heartbreaking episodes in a working life that was gruelling by any standards.

When she came to stay with us – which was often, particularly after her convent moved to Hastings – she would put her work firmly behind her and give her whole attention to her family. Occasionally during her life she needed to get away for a while to rest and recuperate. It was usually to our home in Kent that she came, with her sketch-pad, her paints and her needlework. After her mother died she considered our home as her home, and for that reason we saw her more regularly than the rest of her family did. Of all my father's sisters, she is probably the one I miss the most. I stayed at the Birmingham convent twice, for a few days on each occasion, so I experienced the convent way of life which, in many respects, I suspect was much the same as it was in Poplar, except that there was no longer any nursing.

Aunt Jocey always knew what was going on with each member of her large family, and would find time to visit them all. She even managed to get to Iceland to meet some distant relations. She never forgot to mark a birthday with a hand-drawn or painted card. And in her family there were an awful lot of birthdays to remember! Her many letters often contained humorous drawings too. We always used to wonder how on earth she found the time to do what she did, but now, after reading the books, I'm even more astonished. My memories of Aunt Jocey are mostly from her Hastings and Birmingham days, and I have a vague memory of once going to the Deptford convent, but I would love to know more about the Poplar convent because I live on the Isle of Dogs and am fascinated by its history.

I bought my house on the Isle of Dogs in 1986. Aunt Jocey came here once and was interested to see how the Island had changed and how the riverside had opened up. But there have of course been many more changes since the mid-1980s. Back then, it was a quiet backwater, with no railway, no underground, and no Canary Wharf. There was a single road leading off/on the Island, which was single-track at one point, and the Limehouse Link tunnel did not exist. There were constant smells from the processing plant across the river, and ships' sirens were regularly heard (very seldom now, sadly). In those days, many of the old inhabitants had never ventured off the Island in their entire lives, let alone beyond the East End! It was such a hassle to travel about that people just stayed put. Now the Isle of Dogs has lost much of its distinctive character. Yet a few vestiges remain: near my house is a street that still has prefabs. Every few years one of them collapses and is replaced by a brick version, but half a dozen are still standing. And we still get thick fogs from time to time.

I am intrigued by the fact that you switched from nursing to music. I am a professional singer (www.roddard.co.uk), though I am having to scale this down as I get older, and I play the piano recreationally, though it's hard to find the time to practise. By coincidence, our piano in Kent also dates from 1904. My bread-and-butter work is copy-editing, proofreading and typesetting. I live half the time here in Docklands and half the time at my mother's house in Kent. I would very much like to meet you to discover more about Aunt Jocey's working life, about the Isle of Dogs of the 1950s, and not least about your music. Aunt Jocey was appreciative of music, and she came to many of my concerts, but I don't think she was particularly musical. Having said that, I remember that she was very taken by one particular chant she had heard at Taizé! Her distinctive, slightly breathless way of speaking, and her habit of sounding the 'h' in words like 'which' and 'where' remain forever ingrained in my mind's ear!

With best wishes,
Corinne Orde

'Aunt Jocey', or Sister Jocelyn – Sister Julienne in Call the Mid-wife *– was a key influence on Jennifer – a friend and a confidante, beloved not only by Jennifer but also her family, writing to Jennifer's children and entertaining them with her lively sketches and stories. They maintained their correspondence long after Jennifer's time as a midwife at 'Nonnatus House'.*

St Aidan's Day

Dear Jenny,

Thank you for your letter of August 21st. I am sending this to Boxmoor as I expect you will be back getting ready for school once more by the time this gets delivered. So very glad you and Philip are having (or have had) such a nice time in your Hove flat.

I had not realized Philip painted. Next time we meet I must ask him for some hints!! *Woman's Hour* had a painting competition – the successful entries were to be hung in the Tate in a special two weeks exhibition. The theme was 'Summer Time'.

There were 3,000 entries and 151 were accepted. I was among those who were *not* accepted!! but I had great fun doing the watercolours – but it took me *much longer* to get it mounted and sent off! And for about a month I kept on eagerly hoping! It was worth trying and I must say I prefer my small painting to the two that got first and second prize but that sounds like sour grapes and I am bound to admit, although I *hoped*, I would have been mightily surprised if I had got in! Mother is going to hang my 'Tate reject' in the guest room so it will not be utterly unrecognized!! It was a little watercolour sketch of scarlet poppies growing in a cornfield – I had tried to get a hazy summery day effect of heat with a little breeze that swirled the poppies into dancing attitudes and was quite pleased in the way it had turned out, so that is that!! [That picture hangs to this day in what was Jennifer's bedroom, selected by Jennifer when Sister Jocelyn died.]

Congratulations on getting your Fellowship – that is wonderful news. You have worked so hard and with such joy and dedication that it is good to know you now have recognition and reward – I know what your music means to you and I was *really* delighted to hear that news.

So glad your two returned home safe and sound and more experienced in travel than before – they are growing up so fast now – children no longer. They do credit to you and Philip for they do not seem to have lost the attractiveness and the loving thoughtfulness that young people seem to shed all too quickly and they seem to have so much common sense and responsibility – you have much cause Jenny to thank God as I know you do.

In retreat in June we heard rather a nice story about an overseas Bishop who was so worried about his diocese – he could not sleep: the finance, the clergy, the schools, the church buildings, all came under his worried care. Finally he got up and sat in his chair turning things over and over, then he looked up. God was standing there and God said, 'Get out of that chair and get into bed. I'll sit in the chair and do the worrying, after all it's my world, not yours.' So he went back to bed and slept soundly and God sat in the chair! I think there is a lot of truth in that story – a bit like the storm on the lake with Jesus asleep in the boat.

We had a requiem for your young friend Julian and remembered his parents. I can appreciate all your anguish for them and life does seem strange, as you say. But then life is very full of these happenings. One hesitates to produce 'solutions' to explain it all, I think we just have to look further and deeper *and* closer at our Lord and there the puzzle seems to fit, perhaps not at once, but as one thinks and goes on trusting gradually the glimmering of a pattern begins to show.

I think we do not often appreciate the way we each are linked to others – friends, families, past, present and future and all under God's love. I often think what we like to call coincidence is often just part of this pattern and I certainly think that prayer does not consist of telling God what we need or think others' needs are – as you say, 'perhaps the simple fact that parents instinctively worry is all the prayer that's needed', though I would not myself use the word 'worry'. Love might be substituted, don't you think? Prayer to me seems to be bringing to a Loving Father all our deepest needs for those we love for those who have asked us – and for the world we live in – in *trust* that He knows best.

The more we learn to love and trust Him, the more we find subject matter for prayer. Think of Jesus at prayer in the pages of the Gospel. The power of prayer is tremendous. It is God's prayer and He deigns to use us, His children, if we trust Him. I think that is the vital thing – loving trust. Perhaps difficult to say to a mother who has just tragically lost her child. But no need to *say* it. Our longing to comfort her will be used by God, but in His way, and in the depth of grief and sorrow she will be comforted because some friend has gone in prayer to God for her.

Must end this too lengthy letter.

Much love to you and all,
Jocelyn

7 June

Dear Jenny,

Thank you for your lovely card from St Julian's Shrine. Yes, I remember you went there a while ago – I can see it 'speaks' to you. I was sorry that the opportunity to hear more about it all was not forthcoming. Still, with a daughter in Birmingham, the chance is sure to arise again.

This year has been very 'crammed'! It seems to me we are halfway through it nearly and yet part of it has not been lived through properly yet. If you know what I mean!!? We have had the conferences, a visitation by the Bishop lasting a week! And now on retreat and another conference looming up in the future!!! I'm not grumbling. I think it must be old age.

Sister Audrey told me she once heard old Sister Margaret (now long departed) muttering to herself in the garden at Hastings – 'oh for a little monotony, oh for a little monotony'!! I can almost *hear* your laughter.

> Much love to you and Philip and
> the girls when you next see them,
> Jocelyn

13 December

Dear Jenny,

How very kind and thoughtful you are – I just can't find words to express my delight when I opened your parcel. I was deeply touched by your understanding – just exactly what I was longing for – you have got a big Gift of Generosity – nothing held back – the paints are just super and my fingers are itching to transfer them onto the beautiful paper!!

I have got a lot of Icelandic sketches that I never had either the right paper or the right paint or the right time to work them out to my satisfaction (rather like Alice through the looking glass!!).

Now I am promising myself a real session with your gifts but it will have to wait until after Christmas – however I have all that time to enjoy looking forward to it!! 6–8 hours for painting is not a bit too exorbitant!! And I think Philip has got a *lovely* wife!!!

Dear Jenny, thank you very very much indeed – the brushes, you were absolutely right about – but I have got quite a supply, for down the years I have always cared for them most carefully – some are quite 50 years old or more, and they are all sable – most precious ones – the varnish has come off their handles – but the sable hairs are still as resilient as ever – and their points behave as they should and so you see now with your beautiful present I am all set to work it out of my system, though I am sure it never will get worked out!!!

I feel sure you are absolutely right when you say it was the best decision that was ever made for Philip. Your letter is quite thrilling to read – like Winston Churchill's essay on painting!!

I *do* understand Philip's reactions to payments. I tried to sell some of my paintings at the church Christmas Bazaar – last year the Vicar suggested auctioning one, because he felt I should get more that way – for the congregation are not well off and someone outside might come along, but I just could not bear the idea of it going to someone who did not care very much about it – like a raffle rather, so I know how Philip must feel.

When I was with my sister she introduced me to a great friend of hers who is an artist (amateur) and she was selling her pictures for £40–50 and £60. I asked her how she felt about getting paid and pricing them highly and so on. She replied that if people paid a high price then it meant they liked her pictures! I had not thought about it that way.

I must stop now. I would like to say a lot more about your letter but time does not allow it.

In the words of Jesus, be of good cheer,
Jocelyn

19 September

Dear Jenny,

Thank you very very very much for that really lovely 'surprise parcel'. How very sweet of you to send such lovely thoughtful things. They will be put to use just as soon as I can get to the bottom of a pile of letters patiently waiting to be answered!!!

We also enjoyed your visit *very much* indeed. And we will look forward to you keeping your promise about the harp and the singing.

It was lovely to get up-to-date news of you all and needless to say, we are deeply interested in all your doings. We think especially of Juliette on her return from Australia – and if ever she felt like meeting us tell her to ring us, though we realize that her time will be very fully taken up now.

This comes with much love to you, Philip, Juliette and Suzannah.

I must add how glad I was that you brought over the photographs of Monica and the others too – it really was a lovely day.

Much love again,
Jocelyn

✦

Jennifer also maintained correspondence with another nun of the order, Sister Christine, and visited the community, sending them copies of her books when they came out.

6 December 2007

Dear Jennifer,

Am returning the script of your new book as requested – and I have to say I am really enjoying all that I have read so far. It's so human and 'get-at-able' (if that is a word that can be used).

I think everyone loves to be told stories – and you have 'clothed' the important things you are talking about in stories, so I feel the book will come together well and be really valued. I would love to have it back some time to read again in its entirety.

I have been booked in to have my second cataract done mid-January which will be wonderful as at the moment I find holding focus for any length of time difficult and I'm just longing to get to the point of new glasses and back to the enjoyment of reading with ease and not with a magnifying glass!!

Am about to wrap up the script and take it to the post – but just wanted to say I hope you have a very lovely Christmas.

All the Community send their love and greetings.

My love and prayer to you –
especially for your gift of writing,
Christine

25 June 2009

Dear Jennifer,

Wanted just to say how much we enjoyed seeing you again. Thank you so much for making time to come.

The box of books has arrived safely and we are beginning the enjoyable task of letting people have them for a donation. Your other parcel arrived safely too and our second copy of *Shadows of the Workhouse* is already in the library. Thank you for writing in the book – it makes it special.

We didn't manage to hear you on the radio on Sunday and wondered how you felt it went. On the Saturday thought and prayed for you that it would all go well.

Just wanted to send this little THANK YOU and send love from us all – it's so good to be in contact again.

With my love to you,
Christine

Sister Christine writes about a day in the life of a nun:

I can remember when I first became a Sister, how the structure of the life felt like a pair of very unyielding new shoes that pinched somewhat and certainly weren't at all comfortable. Yet as the years have passed that same structure has given important shape and form to the life I and all my Sisters share. My day starts early at 6.30 a.m. with an hour of personal prayer in chapel. It's a time of deep silence, of making an offering of myself to God, as well as praying for the events of the day ahead and for those who have asked for prayer support. We all bring our prayer together in Morning Prayer at 7.30 a.m.. Praying through the day takes on its own rhythm with the Eucharist at 12.30 p.m., Evening Prayer at 5 p.m. and Compline at 8 p.m. – important times for offering our love and worship and becoming refocused. Each day has its own plan for work and ministry but often unexpected things arise that challenge the best of plans.

Along with Margaret Angela, I am responsible for the administration of the Community, personally being responsible for preparing for Community Conferences when we meet together on Mondays to discuss things that concern us all. Sometimes, like in any family, there are thorny issues that need time and space to work through. Having a new member of the Community who is now starting out on her journey to become a Sister is a joy. Each week we have time together working with the details of her studies. I also have the privilege of walking with people who have asked for someone to accompany them on their journey of faith – that too is a joy – getting to know them well and being able to pray for them each day. There are also those who come distressed for some reason who need to share, where it is important to be able to respond to that immediate need by listening and praying.

Part of the life of any Sister is to help with the 'daily chores' in the house. Every day is different and busy but I know how important it is to put on my apron and roll up my sleeves and share in that part of our life, especially when there are gaps needing to be filled. We have the gift of a day off each week in which to be refreshed and renewed – and when we want to relax I know Margaret enjoys a good read – as for me – give me some flowers to arrange.

Dear Mrs Worth,

Thank you for your letter dated the 15th May which I very much appreciate.

Finished reading your book *Call the Midwife* a few weeks ago, which I thought was excellent. Your story about Mary I thought was particularly sad, and your description of Mrs Jenkins and her children, and what happened to them in the workhouse was very interesting (and very sad).

I try to make your books last as long as possible because I never want them to end.

Picked up your latest book *Farewell to the East End* a few weeks ago from the bookshop. Have read a few chapters and don't have any doubt it's going to be as good if not better than *Call the Midwife* and *Shadows of the Workhouse*.

I was born in a former workhouse in 1944, they demolished it about thirty years ago, and built houses on the site. At the time of my birth it was known as Eaves Lane Hospital, but the place of birth on my birth certificate is 152 Eaves Lane, Chorley.

It's interesting to read about the fifties. One of my memories of the fifties is going with a friend to visit his grandmother. We must have been about ten or eleven. She lived in a little house with a back yard, and when we entered she was sitting in an old rocking chair by the side of the fire. She had a little beard on the end of her chin, and was smoking a pipe, as if that wasn't strange enough, she kept two pigs in the back yard! The back yard was approximately 6' × 12'.

I was brought up in a house with a back yard and they were all similar (minus the pigs). At the end of the yard was an outside 'petty' (toilet) and the other end the kitchen. Placed on top of the toilet roof and kitchen roof, were some old planks of wood under which was the big black pot for boiling up the 'pig-swill', vegetable waste, peelings, etc. We had never heard about health and safety in those days. We used to enjoy going round to our neighbours collecting the waste potato peelings, etc. and stirring the pot of 'pigswill' at my friend's grandmother's.

All the best,
P. Jackson

In reply to a letter from Peter Jackson, Jennifer wrote about just how much the letters she had received from her readers meant to her.

Don't think ever that I 'mind' letters from people like you. I am delighted. They are the most thrilling part of being an author!

26 August 2009

Dear Mrs Worth,

Many thanks for the book dedications which were a very nice thought and greatly appreciated.

Glad you liked the pigs in the backyard story.

I think you'll agree, there were more characters around in the old days. Another 'character' I remember from the fifties was Tommy Smalley who owned a shop (we had five shops in our lane in the fifties, now all gone). He was about 5ft 2ins and had a peg-leg, and he would sell a Woodbine and a match to us kids for 1d.

I have just read your book *Farewell to the East End*, and I wasn't disappointed. It was another excellent book. You should be very proud of all three 'midwife' books and I was thinking what a marvellous television series they would make. The strict order of the nuns and their different characters, the four mid-wives, who sound very different and lively, and the patients and East End characters, ever thought about it?

Good luck, Peter Jackson

Dear Mrs Worth,

I was given your book *Call the Midwife* by my sister who lives in St Albans, and I love it because I too was a midwife in 1944. I did my SRN training in Watford Peace Memorial, did a year staffing and then left to do my midwife in Plaistow, the East End of London and so as you can imagine I had so many experiences like yours while doing my midder that I felt I would love to write and tell you and to say how much I have enjoyed your book.

I have been living in Scotland for quite a few years now, but it was great to read your book and be back again in my 'midder' days even though I'm now 80+ years old!

May I wish you a happy and healthy New Year,
Best wishes,
Gwendoline Hawes

✦

Dear Jennifer Worth,

Having just read your book *Call the Midwife* I was determined to write to you to say how much I enjoyed it and was much moved by it.

You see I also was a midwife in the 50s so it rang so many bells, although your time in the East End presented situations which mine did not.

My training was in Newcastle-on-Tyne and my main area was the Scotswood area. Quite a rough area, but like you, the nurse was respected then, even by drunks. The families I met were poor and hardworking, but I respected and liked them.

That first chapter of yours about the delivery, I was with you all the way. Thank you so much for your experiences laced with humour and sadness. It must have given you a jolt to find yourself in a convent!

Yours sincerely,
Yvonne Fenwick

PS: I look forward to reading *Shadows of the Workhouse* as social history is fascinating.

✦

Memories of midwifery training in Poplar, E14 in 1955–56

District midwifery held far more appeal for me than hospital midwifery. The Nursing Sisters of St John the Divine in Poplar offered pupil midwives six months Part 2 training with deliveries all in the mothers' homes. We lived in the Mission House with the Sisters.

Pupils arrived after passing Part 1 Midwifery Training in hospital. I started in October 1955 with Edith Horton and Pauline Turner. The Sisters welcomed us into their home, came out on cases with us and allowed us to share their community life. I have memories of fun and enjoyment as well as discipline and high standards.

Extracts from some typical case records give glimpses of living conditions in London E14 some sixty years ago.

We cycled everywhere bumping over the cobbles with midwifery bag in front and the 'gas and air machine' (nitrous oxide analgesia) on the back. We were not afraid in the (then) docklands at night. Uniform was respected, the police were helpful. We were sometimes held up if a bridge was opened to allow a tall vessel through.

Newspaper was used to protect furniture. I remember a novice who was overseeing one delivery browsing through the magazine *Reveille* – I teased her about it.

The Sisters were very well respected and appreciated, so we pupils were accepted as part of their service to families.

I did not know Jennifer as I'd left before she came, but I much enjoyed her books and the TV series *Call the Midwife*.

Jo Willoughby, SRN, SCM
QIDNS & HV Tutor

✦

Dear Mrs Worth,

I've read both books. What a wonderful talent you have. Your characters walk off the pages. They are so real and alive, and it would be a hard person who didn't suffer with them. I broke my heart for that little brother and sister. One knew a lot of what went on, nursing in the East End, but being based in a hospital did not let one see all that went on, which you, as a community nurse and midwife, will have experienced.

I was so interested in the Sisters too. Sister Julienne must have been such a wise and deeply spiritual woman. Anglican Sisters find it very hard to keep going. When we meet various Anglican congregations they always say they envy us our back-up, because really they have no one behind them if the bishop or priest isn't keen on nuns.

By writing as you did about Mr Collett you gave him the dignity and recognition which he never received in life. I'm glad you saw him later. We are taught that we will be the age which was the very best for us on earth, so that must have been the age for him. And his words for you could only have come through the One who is Truth itself.

It was interesting to see your picture on the inside cover and to learn that you are a musician. That sensitivity flows over into your writing, and I am so grateful to have the privilege of reading your books and of learning to know you.

Very gratefully,
Sister Elizabeth (Morris)

Sister Elizabeth Morris was the first English girl to enter a German congregation shortly after the war ended. She writes:

There was not one person to encourage me – my relatives were all Anglican and that is a story in itself! All priests said it was a mistake to enter a German congregation. But I know it was what I had to do, for God and for my country, to bring peace and reconciliation.

We are a worldwide congregation but our Sisters here became segregated during the war years, as they were sent over to avoid Hitler. Many also went to Brazil. We have a Mother General with assistants to take overall care of the countries, and local Superiors within the countries themselves.

Her letter to Jennifer Worth was the beginning of a long correspondence and friendship:

Nursing has always been my first love, and for a very short time during the war, I nursed in the London Hospital, and of course saw Jennifer Worth's Sisters on their bicycles.

Years later, in the late 70s, I was a ward sister in St Clement's, Bow, and the Sisters were still cycling around, obviously very much loved and respected. I knew they were midwives, but I didn't know they had a midwifery school.

I love reading about nursing – my first and dearest love – which our Sisters couldn't really understand. When I saw *Call the Midwife* in W H Smith's, and realised the time and the venue, I just had to have it, and all the following books. It was so outstanding I just had to write and thank Jennifer. A strange thing happened. We just seemed to 'click' and we corresponded far more by telephone than the written word, though we wrote to each other several times about her last book. Jennifer was so humble, asking me what I thought, and when I replied that was by letter, because she had written out for me the parts she wished to discuss. We didn't always agree, but we met halfway, and anyway it was *her* book!

When I complimented her on one of her characters she gave

this reply: 'I'm an observer. I didn't want to get too involved. I only got involved once, and I wish I hadn't.'

Now that, of course, was with the old gentleman who died in the home. Jennifer felt too deeply, and suffered with him, as was very clearly portrayed in the television series. She was a sensitive lady, and therefore kept herself at one remove from her patients. That's how she could write with such objectivity.

She phoned me to tell me she was terminally ill, because she didn't want me to read it in the paper. We have never met in flesh and blood, and yet I feel, and I think she did too, that there is a bond between us equal to a friendship of a lifetime. I can never forget Jennifer.

Dear Jennifer,

I know you must have plenty of fan mail as a result of your books about Poplar, but I felt I must drop a line to say how much I enjoyed reading them.

I first heard of your work when listening to a discussion on the radio, and heard the mention of Poplar and 'East India Dock Road'. Being a Poplar lad, born in 1934, and living in Hind Grove for the first twenty-eight years of my life, I immediately pricked up my ears, and decided to buy the books.

I lived in Poplar throughout and after the war, so you can imagine the nostalgia I felt when following your visits around the area. As you rightly say, I remember the people as honest down-to-earth folk who called a 'spade a spade', and what you saw was what you got.

Like all my pals, my grandparents, uncles and aunts, lived round and about, as indeed *their* elders had done before them. So the community was close-knit, and nothing happened without everyone knowing about it. My paternal grandparents lived in Hind Grove for the whole of their married lives, and my father steadfastly refused to move from Hind Grove, even when the 'Planners' bulldozed the road away, forcing my parents to move into Anglesey House (still in Hind Grove). They both died there, aged 82.

Before the days of NHS, when a doctor's visit cost half-a-crown, medical needs were rather ad hoc, as you well know, and my grandma was frequently called upon, day or night, to act as 'Midwife' to neighbours in need, or to 'lay out' the dead when someone had died. Those were the days when a deceased relative was laid out in the 'Parlour' for a week, so that friends and neighbours could pay their respects.

My father and his five brothers were at the old Upper North Street School when it was bombed by a German bomb in June 1917, killing eighteen children, nearly all just 5 years old. Luckily he survived, fathering me to attend the new Upper North Street School throughout the Second World War. You will know that there is a memorial to those deaths in Poplar Recreation Ground in East India Dock Road to this day.

The hub of Poplar was, of course, Chrisp Street Market, where every housewife frequently attended for their shopping needs. In the early days, the market stretched along Chrisp Street itself, with stalls on either side of the narrow road, and the shopping spree often concluded in Cooke's Pie and Mash shop, next to Woolworths.

I remember well my sister's wedding at All Saints Church in 1950. Possibly that church, along with St Anne's at Limehouse, are the only remaining landmarks!

Your pseudonym of Nonnatus House prevents me from identifying your exact workplace, but I do remember the building in Stainsby Road, known locally as 'The Nurses Home', where nurses pedalled off each day to attend their rounds. I feel sure you will be aware of that Home.

My father was well known locally as a DIY man, and I recall a forlorn nurse pushing her bicycle round to our house for him to mend a puncture, which of course he was pleased to do.

Sadly, in the 60s, the words 'Slum Clearance' came into the dictionary, and the 'Planners' were faced with a dilemma: whether to upgrade existing properties, and in-fill the open spaces, or bulldoze the whole area and start again. Sadly (in my view) they chose the latter.

The whole community was scattered to the four winds, never to see each other again, and new high-rise stacks of bricks began to obliterate the character of the whole area. At a stroke, a whole culture was erased as though it had never been. My beautiful Farrance Street School in Piggot Street, with its loft apex roof and two horns on the top, has been obliterated by a façade of blank brick walls. (Now purporting to be luxury flats!) The pubs, where a piano could be heard tinkling out: *My Old Man* . . . and *Show Me the Way to Go Home* have been erased, and the terraced front doors, always held ajar by a coconut mat, have disappeared along with the familiar faces that peered out from behind them.

On a lighter note, I do hope you will dig up more memories of your adventures around Poplar, with a sprinkling of names and places that refugees from Poplar will recall. My cousin, who now lives in Canada, grew up in Maylem Gardens – a row of houses owned by the Gas Works in East India Dock Road. She too enjoys your books, so your fame is now global!

Thanks once again for sharing your memories.

Yours sincerely,
Bill Langworth

Dear Mrs Worth,

Thank you for writing your wonderful books. I cannot tell you how much my wife and I have enjoyed reading them.

I knew absolutely nothing about the work of the Sisters. I knew virtually nothing about the work of midwives. I knew very little about the history of the Docklands, but it is an area I know quite well because of my work as a lorry driver.

As a man, I am afraid I had to skim one chapter in *Call the Midwife* and two chapters in *Farewell to the East End*, but the intricacies of a woman's body are best left as a mystery. Let me explain.

As a boy, I was fascinated by motor vehicles. When I grew older, I learned all about them, but in that process all the magic and mystery was destroyed. Perhaps now you can see why I don't want to learn too much about women, and let them continue to be both magic and a mystery.

You wrote in your chapter 'Adieu' that you owe the Sisters more than you could ever repay. Well, believe me when I tell you you have repaid that debt and then some. I am sure the Sisters of Nonnatus House are looking down on you and must be immensely proud, as must your family and friends.

Your books have stirred up every emotion that I possess, hitherto unparalleled by any non-fictional works I have read. You have a wonderful gift for ending a chapter on a high, humorous or emotional note, if only you could have been employed to read the news!

Thanks to you, I have gained so much knowledge about the people who once lived in the East End. I spend my working life all over the country but there is something uniquely special about those Docklands and I can't quite put my finger on it.

Its air and atmosphere is intense, and you can almost touch its history. It may have been deprived, and may still be, but with different parameters, but it will always be special.

Yours thankfully,
John G. Rooke

Jennifer was very touched by this letter:

Thank you so much for writing to me. You say some lovely things and your writing is almost poetic – the East End of London seems to inspire so many people . . .

John Rooke commented:

Jennifer's books are among our most treasured possessions and the letter she sent is neatly folded in the front cover of our copy of *Call the Midwife* along with some handwritten stickers she kindly sent.

Whoever could have predicted at what point (if ever) the life and career of Jennifer would cross paths with a modern day lorry driver born in 1969?

Between 1998 and 2002, I used to stop at Silvertown, usually 3 nights a week. At that time I worked for Lincoln haulier Geoff Mason & Son. We used to deliver palletised goods around London, then for a 'back load' we would call at Enterprise Forwarding in Aylesford and then on to Gondrand, who used to be located in Oriental Road, Silvertown. Though this was a relatively new warehouse it had a few 'old school' type characters of the East End. I can remember one or two of them recalling how tough their lives had been during their childhood. They were the very same 'little urchins' that Jennifer witnessed running around the cobbled streets and tenement blocks. I recall one of them was a docker's son and lived at 'Custom House' during his childhood. He would be around

62-ish now and could even have been a delivery of the Nonnatus House staff.

There is a certain attitude or way about these characters, they are kind of nonchalant – something to do with the 'make do and mend' attitude perhaps. What was that saying during the war, addressed to Hitler – 'You can bomb our houses, but never our hearts.' These people seemed to me to be different from everyone else, still proud when they 'didn't 'ave a pot to piss in' (excuse my language).

I remember one man I worked with and if ever there was a whip-round for anybody leaving or retiring, there would be a very stern and sharp reply, telling you where to go. However if anyone announced they or their partner were pregnant, he would whip out his wallet and hand over a score (£20) with no questions asked. I think the old East Enders also saw life in black and white – either they liked you or they didn't.

As to me, well I still work as a domestic lorry driver and am away from home 3 or 4 nights a week. I also enjoy writing and drawing and I often reach for my pen or pastels when parked up for the night. My wife is also involved in the road haulage industry, she works in the office of a different haulage firm to me and organises collections and deliveries through a pallet network.

✦

Dear Jennifer – if I may?

I had complex foot surgery a month ago and am learning a lot about temporary immobility. One of the great blessings is that I have the opportunity to read voraciously and am catching up with a backlog of books I have been longing to read for ages!

I have just read *Call the Midwife* and I can't tell you how much I enjoyed it. I was a volunteer in Brick Lane ten years after the time you describe and although there had been many improvements, much of what you describe resonates for me. I didn't go to college or university but I reckon I learnt more valuable lessons for life in the East End.

Years later Father Joe became a dear friend of mine and his son is still a friend now.

So really I just wanted to say a huge thank you for a book I shall long remember with its brilliant mix of humour, tragedy and courage. I hope we meet one day.

All good wishes,
Frances (Sister Frances Dominica)

Dear Mrs Worth,

I have just read your book, *Farewell to the East End*.

The first chapters upset me. I did not think I could continue to read of all the sadness. But I did continue and found it a very good read.

I want to comment on the part about the nurse's time in London as it compares very much with that of an aunt of mine. She went in 1909 to the Salvation Army training home and became a midwife. She too spoke of walking alone to patients, whereas the police always had to go in twos. I recall visiting her at the mother & baby clinic in Hackney where Sister Church was in charge. As an adjutant and nurse in the Salvation Army she wore not an Army bonnet but a type of small skullcap with a broad navy ribbon scarf with plum, blue and yellow stripes hanging down her back. She retired with ill health in 1933 and came to live with us – I was seven years old.

Thank you for allowing me to see her life as your book unfolded.

J. H.

Dear Mrs Worth,

My name is Frances and I am a member of a reading group of 8 women who meet monthly. We are aged between 40 and 60, from different backgrounds and professions, most with, but some without, children. We all are united in the fact that we loved your book *Call the Midwife* and have voted it our most favourite book so far! We were enthralled by the stories which have brought so much interesting discussion to the group. We keep coming back and talking about it and are all gradually reading the next two books which are equally as compelling.

Your descriptions were so good that you could feel when reading you were actually there. How things have changed and moved on. Personally I couldn't put the books down and look forward to reading your next (fourth) book.

My parents were both in the medical profession. My mother was a midwife and my father a GP who trained at the London Hospital just before the war. They met at King George's Hospital in Ilford and my father worked at the surgery in Woodford Green for over 40 years.

My twin brother and I were born by emergency Caesarean at the London Hospital in 1960. My mother and her midwife were both convinced she was having twins but the doctor said 'No'. He should have listened to the experts!

It seems to me that the most interesting stories come from real-life experiences. You have inspired me to get on and start writing the book I keep talking about.

With best wishes and many thanks,
Frances Trenouth and Trevone Readers Group

Jennifer was delighted with this letter and replied:

. . . a letter like yours is worth all the reviews – better, in fact. Keep writing – there is a big interest in real-life stories these days, unusual, funny, sad, anything *real*, and such experience can only be gained from life. I didn't know I could write until I started.

✦

Dear Jennifer,

I hope you won't mind me writing to you like this. I was given your book *Call the Midwife* for Christmas by a friend. It was of great interest to me as I was working on the District Midwifery team at the London Hospital in the 1950s. Our area was a mile radius of the London, so we must have overlapped with you in lots of areas. I had no idea that there were other midwives in that area.

Your book brought back so many memories. We lived in a house in Turner Street. Sister Haynes was in charge of us, we had all completed our training but it was my first post as a Certified Midwife. I had completed the first part of my training at the London and the second part in Gloucester. My home was a little village in Suffolk so like you it was a complete culture shock for me. I delivered babies in a brothel, the Tower of London, Blackwall buildings that were terrible places, and in Brick Lane on a Sunday morning with the market going on outside the window.

Sister Haynes ruled with a rod of iron, but she was a wonderful Christian lady. Those of us who were committed Christians had to attend church every Sunday. When she had a weekend off she would ask the chaplain if we had been. I can't imagine young women putting up with that in these days. Sister had been there all during the war and I am sure would have been able to tell some tales.

Sometimes riding a bike at night could be scary but we always had a medical student with us. The bikes also had THE LONDON HOSPITAL painted on them and the hospital was so respected in the area we felt safe.

I haven't written anything down but I do give talks in the

area to local clubs. It always amazes me how having a baby brings so much interest and discussion.

If you were not too busy I would love to know if you knew of our existence in Turner Street. You might even have known Sister Haynes.

Yours sincerely,
Jill Fryer-Kelsey

The following extract is from a history Jill Fryer-Kelsey wrote for her children:

Sister Gladys Haynes was in charge of the four of us who were all State Certified Midwives. I was the junior, the newest qualified. We all had our own room which among other things had a point to plug in the telephone when we were the first on call at night. Being woken at 3 a.m. by the porter in the main hospital telling you that Mrs Jones was in labour in such and such a street, and did you know where that was, was quite daunting until you got used to it. The London Hospital had a system which entailed a white card which the husband or friend brought to the reception. If you didn't know where the street was the husband would wait for you and take you there. Sister Haynes had been there during the war and told this story. She was following a husband and she thought he was going through an underpass but too late found out that it was the men's toilet!

After breakfast each day we had a staff meeting to discuss the day's calls and get an update on any new arrivals. For the daily visits we had a chauffeur-driven car which looked very official, especially when we had to drive into the Tower of London.

The Tower of London was in our district, there were servicemen and their families living in apartments. In the early hours of the morning I was called out to a mum in labour. The problem with the Tower was having to have a password to get the gates open at night. The husband was there to let us in but because the password had to be changed each time we came and went, it was easier to stay there – which turned out to be a long time.

Wapping was sometimes difficult to get to when the bridges were up. Our drivers tried to beat the boats coming up and get to the next bridge before it went up! Delivering a baby in the Customs House which was right by the Thames was an experience. The mother's contractions stopped and she fell asleep. The student and I sat there quietly when suddenly the room began to shudder and there was this very loud throbbing noise outside, when I looked out there was the top of a big ship going past the window. It turned out to be the pleasure boat coming back from Southend. The mum was obviously used to this as she never stirred. These apartments were quite luxurious as they had indoor toilets and baths; they also had lifts to the various floors.

In contrast Blackwall buildings were the worst. The stairs up were on the outside and were open metal. In the winter they were often icy and in the summer the local children would delight in looking up our skirts! Four flats on a landing would share a tap and a toilet. However the resourceful East End ladies managed to keep them clean and tidy.

It was a very hot summer when I was there; often windows in the rooms wouldn't open but when they did there was little fresh air. Delivering a baby close to the Royal Mint, I opened the window only to find I was looking into a large noisy room where notes were rolling off a press. They were suffering with the heat too and I suppose working with all that money would make you hot under the collar!

I was called out in the middle of the night to an unbooked case. It was in one of the seedier areas of the district so I was glad I had one of the medical students with me. The student carried the gas and air machine on his bike and the midwives took the delivery bag. Everything we needed was in that bag. We only asked the family to supply a pile of old newspapers, a clean sheet, a towel to wrap the baby in and two pots, one for hot water and one for cold. As this was unbooked we hadn't visited to see if they had these things. When we arrived I was horrified to find that I was in a brothel! It wasn't the most comfortable situation and I was glad it was a quick delivery.

The uniform at the London was quite old-fashioned even in the 1950s. The dresses were gathered into a yolk and then again into the waistband, which didn't do much for your figure. The sleeves were puffed and were starched in the hospital laundry so they stuck up all the time. Our outdoor coats had the same puff sleeves to accommodate them. Our outdoor hats could only be described as pork pies!

When I married in 1959 I had to leave the district post and as my husband and I were living in Hampstead I went to work at Queen Mary's maternity home, which was an annex of the London Hospital, until I started my own family.

10 June 2008

Dear Mrs Worth,

I have just finished reading your book *Call the Midwife* and I am writing to you for two reasons: firstly, I was a district midwife in the 1950s but working in the back-to-back bombed areas of Birmingham. I am often recounting my experiences of those days and friends have said 'you should write a book' but I never seem to have had the time or know-how. I really relived those days as I read.

The second reason is more interesting, I think. We have an elderly lady in the village who was a young woman in her twenties during the war and she has told me how she dropped by parachute into France during the war dressed as a nun. She carried with her a missal or breviary, to give more authenticity to her disguise if she was captured. This missal had belonged to a Sister Evangelina who I think she said had worked in the East End of London. This lady had also been a nurse and I have told her about your book but she cannot read it for herself because she is now blind. The last few years she has started to talk about some of her exploits as she is now free from the Secrets Act. She will not tell all because some of the people concerned are still alive and it would encroach upon their privacy.

I wonder if you think your Sister Evangelina might be the one connected to Margaret's bravery during the war? She would, I am sure, love to know.

My best wishes with your next book.

Yours sincerely,
Marjorie E. Lambert

Jennifer Worth telephoned Marjorie Lambert soon after she received her letter. Marjorie writes:

I was very surprised to hear from her at all and extremely surprised that she telephoned so soon. We were on the telephone for ages having a wonderful conversation, exchanging stories and laughing together. I laughingly told her 'you have pipped me to the post, I had started to think about a book.'

Marjorie shares these memories of her time in nursing and as a midwife:

When I trained it was usual to train as a nurse, get some experience and then go on to do some midwifery. After four years at UCH in London I took an interim post for a short while as a nurse at Avery's. I then started my midwifery training at Cambridge. At that time the training involved two parts of six months each. Many people only did Part 1 and then returned to General Nursing. I elected to do Part 2 in Birmingham, the first half was in hospital and the second half in the community. This was an eye-opener for me. I had led a pretty sheltered life apart from the bombing until I went to UCH London to train as a nurse and even this was quite sheltered. A few patients came in smelly and dirty but this was soon rectified.

The area I worked in was one of the slum areas not demolished by Hitler. My first initiation was to find out where people lived. Most of the housing of the district consisted of back-to-back houses surrounding a courtyard with a row of toilets at one end. Each toilet was shared by several families, each family having a key. The first mistake I made was to knock at what was the front door, only to be told you need the back house love. Many of the toddlers just ran around in a vest. Everywhere seemed grey but I in my uniform of green hat and gabardine coat, carrying a steel black case, was always treated as a friend. I soon learned to just open the door, call out and go in.

One funny thing happened concerning the gas and air machine. We used cycles so could not carry these. They were left on the step for the husband to collect. One night I sent the husband as usual, but he was ages; in fact by the time he arrived back with it the baby was safely in the cot. I asked in no uncertain terms where he had been and he told me the police had made him open the case containing the machine and they could not get it all back in!

I worked in three different areas. One was near the canal and I delivered on a barge, another time the furniture I had seen when I visited antenatally had disappeared and I delivered on a mattress on the floor. But in spite of everything I loved my time in the community and only had to leave it and return to the hospital because of ill health caused by the conditions I worked in. I went on to teach midwifery students and then back to nursing to teach the teachers.

I believe I came across the order of nuns that Jenny worked for whilst working in Birmingham. One day I remember calling in to see someone postnatally. The house was not clean but there was the husband on his hands and knees with bucket and scrubbing brush and a small nun standing over him with hands on hips . . .

✦

5 January 2004

Dear Ms Worth,

I am writing to thank you for your most excellent book, *Call the Midwife*, which I was given at Christmas.

I couldn't put it down as it reminded me so much of the six happy months I spent with the Sisters in the early sixties, although in their other house in Deptford.

We cycled to the Poplar side via the Greenwich foot tunnel for teaching sessions with those your side of the river. Our clinic was opposite the public cleansing station where many a time we had to redirect the unfortunate men from the nearby massive men's hostel, which coped with 'travellers' from the south-east of England.

The only colleague I was in touch with for many years unfortunately died in her early 50s but I am still very much in touch with her identical twin sister who visited us often. She did her midder with the Salvation Army slightly north of you. I have suggested that she reads the book as I'm sure she will enjoy it too.

I am enclosing copies of photos taken at the time. As you see, the bomb sites were still there ten years after your experiences.

Once again, many thanks for helping me relive some very happy memories.

Yours faithfully,
Marian J. Smith (Miss)

Marian Smith added:

My main off-duty task was to repair the bicycles' punctured tyres as they had to last as long as possible. Our uniforms were gabardine macs and berets. Every so often we had a jumble sale where we also sold articles we had knitted in our Sunday afternoon, very relaxed time with the Sisters. These sales were quite an experience as when we opened the doors, it seemed that the whole of Deptford poured in, but the money was needed.

The Sisters were kind and caring but also full of fun. We played a prank on them and they responded with one on us.

15 November 2008

Dear Jennifer,

Please are you the Jenny Lee I met once at the Mission House in Lodore Street, Poplar, with the Nursing Sisters of St John the Divine?

I've just read your book *Call the Midwife* with very great interest and pleasure. I was thrilled to read your book, as I soon realised the pseudonym could only be for NSSJD! What memories it brought back to me of my days there. It was only when you mentioned the phone call from your friend calling 'Jenny Lee' that I thought, I'm sure that name rings a bell. And didn't I once visit you in a room you had at the other end of the corridor to me, on the lay Sisters and pupils' floor of the Mission House? But you may not remember me. Perhaps you were only visiting then as I don't remember you at meals, etc. Maybe you were already at the London Hospital working? It is all a bit vague to me now after so many years and so much happened since!

I am amazed at your memory. I couldn't possibly remember in such detail! What an amazing story about Len and Conchita Warren and their 25 children!!! And not one of them lost – even that little last one born so prematurely in the ghastly London smog. I must have been at Guy's then doing my general training as I remember the smogs only too well – especially one very bad one. I was so fascinated by your detailed descriptions of everything – that breach delivery too – was that Sister Madeleine with you? – who was the tutor at Deptford when I knew her; she certainly was an exceptional woman. Sister Jocelyn was in charge at Poplar when I went – maybe 1959 or '60 or '61? I was only with them for 18 months before I went to the Community of the Sisters of the Love of God at Fairacres,

Oxford, in September, 1961 where I was professed in temporary vows, but left before taking final vows to follow a further hermit vocation. So I gave up nursing after Poplar and have lived a life of prayer ever since.

I didn't recognise the Sisters you describe, but I did Mrs B. That was Mrs Barnes? She was very fond of me, so I don't remember her telling us all not to mess her kitchen!! But we do all remember different things, don't we? I had some good laughs I can tell you. Father Joe Williamson came to Fairacres while I was still there to talk to us and visit one of our Sisters he'd rescued from the streets!! I only knew her history when I left because I followed her in the Community – but she is a lovely friend of mine still and a brilliant scholar also! Also Tony his son came to talk to us when standing for election so I was interested to see he is now a Canon and President of the Wellclose Trust.

Thank you so much for writing that very interesting, well written, remembered book. My next door neighbour here, with two young children, was complaining to me of her house being too small! So I mentioned the 'Single-ends' of Glasgow slums I'd worked in, families all in one room with no mod cons and in the East End of London! That is how the book came into my hands. Eileen said, 'Oh, have you read the midwife's book?' And it went into my letterbox next day! The next day I caught her again on her way out and told her the book was about where I'd worked! So she was thrilled about that too and it will now 'go the rounds' of the mums here!

All the best, Jennifer and many thanks for a book none of us can hardly put down!

Nancy E. Bacon

Nancy writes that Jennifer did indeed remember her. In fact, she said:

'. . . of course she could remember me, vividly', even my voice, though when we spoke later on the phone that had changed a bit – but my laugh at one point brought out a ready response her end of 'oh yes! That is the laugh I remember' . . . She told me she kept a low profile while I was around, being in awe of me somewhat – being a trained midwife – and I suspect she had suffered from Nursing Sisters in the past! But in Scotland where I trained in midwifery we were all treated as trained, qualified nurses – all much the same. So of course that is how I treated pupil midwives who came out with me on cases. But Jenny was never a pupil who came out with me . . .

Jenny very kindly also sent me her subsequent books as they were published and I learnt a lot more from her research. *Shadows of the Workhouse* was a revelation – I knew the woman who was born there and worked with the Sisters. I met her first at Hastings where the Mother House then was, and later at Poplar. I remembered her differently to Jenny as I didn't remember her awkwardness. But I wish I had known her background at the time as it would have helped to understand her. I was always a bit puzzled about her, though we got on well enough.

When Jenny was writing her last book *In the Midst of Life* she asked for our prayers and we were in touch a number of times over the years. So I knew her better latterly than when we were together in Poplar. She also knew how silly she had been to be in any awe of me at Poplar!

With the publication of *In the Midst of Life* and the gift of that book then came her phone call to tell me of her inoperable cancer and her wish for no invasive treatment. And her family then took over her wonderful care so she could die in peace. Hers was a completed life and she has left a wonderful legacy of interest and help to others. Little do we really know the many people we meet in life. Some more than others, of course, but it was a privilege to 'meet' Jenny again and get to know her properly this time.

Dear Jennifer Worth,

I'm writing to tell you how much I have enjoyed reading your book, *Call the Midwife*.

I'm a midwife, now living and working in Australia. I trained in Central London in the early 1980s and remember the Peabody Buildings.

I worked briefly at St Pancras Hospital, once a workhouse – and was fascinated by your experiences in the East End.

I've always been sceptical about the 'old ways' being natural and safer for women that current midwives in the Home Birth movement enthuse about and found your account very interesting, especially working without oxytocin injections.

I'm looking forward to reading your next book and am much intrigued by your tantalising glimpses of Paris!

Yours sincerely,
Sally Gregor

Paris Interlude

by Jennifer Worth

After qualifying as a nurse and before proceeding with her mid-wifery studies, Jennifer took some time out in Paris. This material is previously unpublished.

Paris in the 1950s

How did Paris of the 1950s, from which I was recently returned, compare with London of the same time? Both great cities had been ravaged by war; both proud independent populations had suffered hundreds of thousands dead or missing. A shattered economy, a shattered culture.

I was lucky. I was there in Paris, young, vital, alive and alert, open to everything that came my way. I adored just walking alone, mile after mile, through that historic city. The great boulevards, the majestic squares, the squalid back streets, the beautiful, silent river. When you are young, everything is beautiful.

Who today can imagine Paris without cars? That was the first thing I noticed. The street cafés spread their tables way out into the road, because cars were so few, and you could sit there half the day and find that only half a dozen small rackety Citroëns or Renaults would pass you. London had always been busy with lorries and heavy goods vehicles, because London was a port, one of the greatest commercial ports in the world. There were few privately owned cars in London at that time, but plenty of lorries. Paris was blissfully free of both.

Can you imagine today strolling diagonally across the Place de la Concorde, or Place Vendôme, gazing at the lovely architecture, day-dreaming? You could set up a stool and easel, and many artist students actually did that, right in the middle of la Place, and were perfectly safe. If a car did come along, the driver would sound a long aggrieved wail on his hooter, but he would drive around you, gesticulating with both hands, and shouting loud Gallic curses. Gendarmes would sometimes try to move an artist on, and I have stood in the middle of la Concorde, trying desperately to control my laughter, while authority and an outraged youth battled it out verbally. Usually authority won, because they would carry vicious-looking batons and were not above using them. But a beguiling artist, determined in his right to produce his masterpiece wheresoever he chose, and calling upon his liberté and egalité as justification, not to speak of his fraternité with Renoir, Cézanne, Monet, was sometimes allowed to remain. When a gendarme appeared, though, I generally made myself scarce, because they were tough, unsmiling men, armed to the teeth with menacing-looking guns, and if they suspected a young foreigner was standing nearby laughing, they might have taken it as a personal insult.

Imagine those tree-lined boulevards, those majestic squares, which today are merely car parks, when they were traffic-free. I think the breathtaking grandeur of the squares is one of the things I remember most and the click-click of a woman's high heels on the pavement, or the bang of a large front door shutting across the other side of the square. Imagine the sound of sparrows squabbling for the crumbs thrown to them. Or your eye being drawn upwards by the sound of a window opening, so you continue gazing up at the balconies, the balustrades, the stone carvings, the crazy conglomeration of chimney pots. You tend not to notice these things when a square has been reduced to the level of a car park.

Another thing that I remember most clearly, and noticed with surprise at the time, was the absence of bomb sites. London was a devastation of bomb sites, and I suppose I had just grown used to it and accepted it as normal, as young people everywhere do, therefore I expected Paris to be the same. I had overlooked the fact that London had been subjected to merciless bombing during the war, whereas Paris had not. Paris had been an occupied city from about 1940, and had remained under German denomination until liberation in 1944, so obviously no German bombs had been directed at a city which housed tens of thousands of German troops. The city had suffered in other ways, though, from grenades, shells, shoot-outs, and the inhabitants had suffered most dreadfully, but the buildings had been spared wholesale destruction.

Fog was another thing I missed! Fog was an accepted fact of life in London. Before the Clean Air Act, it hung over the city a great deal, sometimes as smog, which killed thousands each winter. It was not generally regarded as a blessing. However, these things depend upon your point of view. The Frenchman Claude Monet is on record as saying during one of his stays in England in 1899: 'Without fog, London would not be a beautiful city. It is fog that gives London its magnificent breadth.'

'Oh to see ourselves as others see us.' There are about twenty lovely paintings by Monet of London in the fog, and there is no doubt that he got it right. Without the foggy quality, these pictures would be dull and ordinary.

Bonjour Paris

How did I come to be in Paris? After three and a half gruelling years of nurse's training at the Royal Berkshire Nursing Hospital, Reading, subjected to the iron discipline of the nursing hierarchy of those days, I was aching for freedom and movement. Also I wanted to learn French. Nursing is a universal skill, but without the language, I could not apply for a job in a French hospital so domestic work was the only option.

There were no au pair agencies in those days, so I inserted a small advert in *Le Figaro* stating that a British trained nurse, experienced with children, was seeking a job in Paris. I had about forty replies – all in French. That was a bit tricky, but a friend spoke the language fluently, and he agreed to sort the letters, translate them, and write a reply.

We met and he took me out to dinner at the best hotel

in Henley where the dining room overlooks the Thames. We entered, a grey-haired scholarly-looking gentleman, with a tall slender girl, radiant with happiness, at his side. The dining room was full, and discreetly quiet in the way the English like to enjoy their evenings – a soft hum of conversation, the chink of cutlery on china, the movement of a chair. As we followed the head waiter to our table, I said in a voice that was probably too loud: 'When we've had our meal, I want you to look through all these French letters and pick out the best.' I wondered why he gasped and looked uncomfortable all evening. It was a long time before I found out the other meaning of 'French letters'!

In the event, I went to a family in the Neuilly quarter, near the Pont de Neuilly, Île de Puteaux, just north of the Bois de Boulogne. Monsieur and Madame B had six children, the eldest fourteen, the youngest aged two, and they lived in a large old house set within high brick walls. At the entrance was a small gatehouse wherein dwelt a very old woman who acted as a sort of concierge and who was known to everyone as 'la vieille'. She knitted for the children and mended their clothes, and took in the milk and the post. She peeled the vegetables, sitting on the cobbles of the courtyard. She fascinated me. I never knew her name or spoke to her, but I watched her. Her little claw-like hands gathering up a few onions; her downcast eyes, with quick suspicious upward glances; her habit of shuffling along close to a wall, as though trying to blend into it; all spoke of a person born into servitude in the nineteenth century, of surviving two world wars and about ten years of enemy occupation, and throughout, endless grinding poverty. She was treated with great kindness by the family, and the children were clearly fond of her. Often there is a bond between the very old and the very young. I watched her sitting on a stool in the sun, her back pressed hard against the secure enclosing wall of the courtyard, sucking her stumpy clay pipe and muttering to herself. The little two-year-old would toddle up, and gravely give a stone, which she received with a toothless chuckle. She was enjoying a halcyon old age.

The Bs were a happy, loving family and treated me with great courtesy. I got on well with the children, though the little ones found it very odd that I couldn't understand them and said to one another '*elle est folle*' (she's mad). Mme B arranged for me to go to L'Alliance Française each afternoon and my life slipped into a comfortable routine of child-minding in the mornings and language classes in central Paris in the afternoons, after which I was free to wander around the city for an hour or two.

Beside me, and *la vieille*, the family kept a maid referred to as *la bonne*. She was a buxom, vigorous, happy-go-lucky type called Rosa. She came from an Italian peasant family who had been displaced during the war, and found themselves near Paris. Rosa worked from early morning to late at night, seven days a week. She had no time off during the day, and only one Sunday off per month.

Sometimes when I was still in bed, I would hear her creeping down at about five in the morning to start work in the kitchen, and often it was midnight before she climbed the ladder to the attic where she slept. It really was an attic, because I went up there once – full of old boxes and suitcases and discarded family clutter. No chair or wardrobe. No window or light. Just a bed.

But Rosa didn't appear to mind. She always seemed happy. She did all the cooking, she waited at table, did all the shopping, the housework, the washing and ironing. And all the while she sang. I listened enchanted to her strong, vigorous soprano voice singing as a bird does for the sheer joy of it. She sang Italian opera, Neapolitan songs, Venetian gondola songs, French popular songs, American songs. She filled the house with music, and the children loved her.

I liked her. We couldn't talk to each other because her French was not very good, and mine was non-existent, but that didn't matter. As the weeks passed and my French got a bit better, we communicated more, and she asked me if I would like to join her on her monthly visit to her family the following Sunday. I accepted with pleasure. It was a grave mistake.

Late November can be bitterly cold in Paris, and it was 6.00 p.m. before we left, as Rosa had to work all Saturday. We took the tram out of the city, then a branch line train to heaven knows where, then a two-mile walk through muddy lanes beneath dripping trees. I, like a fool, had dressed up for the occasion as it was my first weekend invitation and I carried a smart little overnight case, containing a stylish change of clothes. I had not realised we were heading for a chicken farm. In actual fact, the farming of the chickens, and the dwelling of the family was very much the same: a collection of tin and asbestos shacks in the middle of a waterlogged field.

The family greeted Rosa with joy. She was showered with hugs and loud kisses and a wave of noisy Italian. The family consisted of her father, mother, grandfather, and three brothers and a sister all in their twenties. None of them spoke any French, because they all worked with the chickens, and Rosa was the only one who lived away from home. The family were very kind, and tried their best to be hospitable and welcoming, but with no way of communicating, and probably not much in common, it was heavy going. Knowing that I would be in their midst for twenty-four hours, I felt uncomfortable, and wondered how I was going to get through it.

It was about eight-thirty when we arrived, and it was very hot in the large square room with corrugated tin walls and ceiling, set on a raised wooden floor. The heat came from a large coke stove, which was also the oven. A delicious smell arose from it. The family had been awaiting our arrival before eating, because hardly had we taken off our coats, than Rosa's mother pulled a big table from the side of the room over to the fire, and glasses were brought out. Chairs and boxes and benches were assembled, and we all sat down, nine to the table. Amid cheers, a huge dish of spaghetti was carried proudly to the table, and a saucepan of gorgeous smelling sauce was poured over it and mixed in. Glasses were filled to overflowing with a nameless red wine, and everyone shouted and toasted each other and drank deeply. Then they each grabbed a fork, and attacked the dish. I mean that literally – they all ate from the central bowl, with great speed and gusto, scooping up forkfuls of spaghetti, slurping it down, and biting off stray ends and letting them fall back into the dish. Their heads were all close, and they grinned and winked at each other as they slurped and scooped. I gazed at the scene in horror and at my fork in dismay. It did not take long to work out that if I was going to get anything at all to eat that night, I would have to stake a claim. I was hungry. I had not eaten for about eight hours, and had had a two-mile walk in the rain. Besides which, the food smelt delicious. Gingerly I leaned forwards, and stuck my fork in. Nothing happened. I tried again. It all just slid off. It may seem funny today, when foods are virtually international, but I had never seen spaghetti before, much less tried to eat it. I made a third attempt, with no success. Everyone was chomping great mouthfuls of the stuff, but I could get nothing, and the dish was rapidly emptying.

Rosa must have seen the dismay and bewilderment on my face, for she gave a great scream of laughter, and waved to everyone to stop eating. Then she very kindly explained to me that you have to twirl the fork around, and hold your face close to the dish in order to scoop the spaghetti into the mouth. She invited me to have a try, and they all sat back to watch. I felt very self-conscious, but their laughter was obviously not unkind. I twirled and twirled, with no success, and eventually in desperation got my fingers in to help the pasta onto the fork. Everyone cheered as it entered my mouth, with bits of sauce flying all over my face and blouse. Then they all fell to again, assuming that my troubles were over.

The meal went on and on. Another huge vat of spaghetti was strained – steam flooding the room – and poured into the dish, which was as big as a washing-up bowl. More spaghetti, more sauce, more wine in an endless flow. I began to feel more comfortable, helped by the wine, and soon I was scooping and twirling and slurping with the ease of the others. The only thing I missed was the conversation, but that didn't really matter. The talk was loud and laughter filled the room. I could not understand a word, but from their expressions, the winks, the gestures, I gathered it was pretty bawdy. Then they started singing. None of them sang as well as Rosa, although the men were surprisingly good, and were more or less in tune. They sang Neapolitan love songs, until tears streamed down the mother's face. I joined in. I did not know the words of the songs, but I have a good ear for music, and could weave a harmony or counter-melody around the melodic line. My voice was a good match for Rosa's, and together we kept up a stream of song, getting more and more sentimental as the evening blended into night. I enjoyed it: a wonderful evening, good food, good wine, good company, music – what more could you ask?

During the course of the evening, each of the men had got up and gone outside, to return a few minutes later. I knew what that meant – an outside lavatory. I looked at the steady rain. Also, when one of the men returned, a couple of cats streaked in as the door opened. One of them was caught and hurled out, but the other remained hidden somewhere. I looked around with dread in my heart. Cats will provoke an asthma attack for me. As the evening wore on, several other cats sneaked in from the rain. I did not know how many were in the room hiding under the furniture or behind the stove, but my anxiety was mounting.

Eventually it was agreed that we should go to bed. I reckon we were all pretty drunk. Rosa grinned apologetically to me that we would have to go outside to relieve ourselves. There was no alternative, so I followed her. It was pitch-black outside, and the soggy mud was treacherous. Rosa led me about fifty yards from the huts, and as my eyes became accustomed to the dark, I could see ahead a little: two posts, about six foot high, placed about four or five feet apart. This was the lavatory, just a hole in the ground. Now it's all very well for a man to pee into a hole, but it's not so easy for a lady! I had to squat over that stinking hole in the rain, hanging on to the posts for dear life, terrified that I would slip and fall in.

Back in the warmth, I saw that about three or four bedrooms led off the main room, and the party was breaking up. I didn't know where I was to sleep, and it seemed neither did anyone else. There was some conversation and then Rosa came up to me, and in very correct French, asked me if I would like her brother for the night. The oldest brother stood beside her. He was about thirty, powerful, dirty and unshaven but confident in his virility. Many girls would have jumped at the chance of a big buck Italian man for the night, but not me. I had to think quickly. I smiled sweetly and, in my very best French, I thanked him but said no, there was an Englishman whom I loved and whose honour I would not betray. Rosa translated and he accepted my response absolutely. He just said '*peccato*!', shrugged and walked off.

Eventually we all retired. The grandfather slept in the main room on the floor, by the stove, and he was already snoring. It was arranged that I was to sleep with Rosa and one of her younger brothers. She took me into the bedroom, which was a tiny cabin only just large enough to take a double bed. This was crammed up against the walls on three sides, leaving about six inches between bed and wall on the fourth side. The space was so narrow that I had to shuffle along sideways beside the bed. There was no light. It was freezing cold and damp in the room, and I felt my lungs contract with the sudden change of temperature. I knew it would be a bad night.

A real asthma attack can be a frightening experience and in those days there was no relief beyond ephedrine tablets – which I did not have – keeping warm, and doing breathing exercises. I quickly abandoned the idea of putting on my nightie, and instead put on an extra jumper, and pulled my coat around my shoulders. The blankets felt damp and stiff, and the eiderdown was stuffed with feathers. There was one feather pillow available. Knowing I would have to sit up all night, I grabbed the pillow and put it lengthways up my back, so that I was sitting upright, leaning against the wall. I sat there in silence for a few minutes, leaning forwards, doing my breathing exercises, as I had seen my grandmother and my mother doing, since earliest childhood. I was coughing badly, my lungs were on fire, and I knew there would probably be no sleep for me that night.

Rosa and her brother came in laughing, and crawled over me to the far side of the bed, the brother in the corner, and Rosa in the middle. They didn't seem to notice that I was sitting upright, or that my breathing sounded like a steam engine. Perhaps they put it down to English eccentricity. Within seconds they were both sound asleep.

I sat there for many hours, leaning forwards on my knees, counting to steady my breathing – ten in, hold for twenty, ten out. Keep it slow, don't panic, don't move suddenly, just keep breathing slowly and regularly, and the attack will pass. I heard owls and animals scuffling outside. Probably rats, I thought. That must be why they kept so many cats. I heard the grandfather getting up and shuffling about, raking out the stove, and tipping in more coke. I heard the sounds of my own breathing subside; the asthma was passing, and I was able to lean back against the pillow and doze.

Somehow, don't ask me how, I got through the night. The breakfast was good – hot chocolate in a huge shallow cup which warmed the hands as well as the stomach, delicious bread that had been rising on the stove all night, and was baked that morning by Rosa's mother. She was very kind, but all she would say to me was 'chow?' and I smiled and replied, 'si, chow'. The men took no notice of me, for which I was grateful. Rosa got up about midday. We had an excellent spaghetti lunch, and left about 4.00 p.m. to return to Paris.

It was destined that I should spend only six more weeks with the Bs, which was very sad because I liked them, and they liked me. Monsieur acquired for me several tickets for L'Opéra Comique and some symphony concerts. Madame introduced me to her circle of friends who I found interesting but even more class-conscious and snobbish than English circles of the time. The children were well brought-up and intelligent, and nice to be with. But it all came to a sudden end when a good-natured exchange with an Algerian boy led to a misunderstanding with the family. I was told to pack my bags and find a new job as quickly as possible.

Encore Paris

I was lucky. It was not difficult to find another placement as a nanny. In fact it was a buyer's market. Wealthy Parisiennes were all looking for servants of one sort or another at that time, and I was able to take my pick. As soon as I said that I was an English trained nurse, and showed my certificate, no one asked for a reference, such was the immediate respect for English nurses.

I accepted a place with a young couple who had just had their first baby. They lived in a magnificent apartment just off the Place de l'Étoile.

It proved to be the perfect job because there was almost nothing to do! After years of working a ten-hour day for six days a week, a life of leisure and pleasure offered its charms. Madame had had her first baby and wanted to spend all her time with him. Two grandmothers were also in daily attendance, and several aunts regularly came and went. What could be left for me to do? Perhaps I was only employed for the prestige, so that they could boast to their friends that they had an English nurse. Whatever the reason, I was gloriously free!

I continued to attend L'Alliance Française for lessons and it provided friends, chief amongst them a beautiful German girl called Helga. Helga gathered artists around her like a flower gathers bees. She was very artistic, but not an artist; very intelligent, but not formally educated; very musical, but not a trained musician; sympathetic, sensitive, generous. It seemed to me that half the young artists of Paris were in need of food, which she provided; in need of shelter, which she offered; in need of canvas or paint, which she procured; in need of admiration and criticism, which she gave in long hours of earnest conversation, sitting in the cafés drinking strong black coffee and cheap red wine. She obviously had a great knowledge of art, and would study a canvas for twenty minutes or so, and then, gravely and kindly, point out this or that tiny detail to the eager young artist awaiting her verdict. For one who has no eye for visual art, it was deeply interesting, and without Helga's friendship, I would never have been introduced into the painters' circles.

Were any of them great artists? I could not say. The Montmartre of around 1900 is now famous for artists such as Picasso, Chagall, Toulouse-Lautrec, Matisse and others. Montmartre of the 1950s had no artists with such fame and influence, but after the war the quarter had reassumed its Bohemian vigour. Life seemed to be lived in the streets. Every shop was either an artists' supplier's, a bistro, a tabac, a bookshop, or a business related to food – pâtisseries, charcuteries, boulangeries, crèmeries and boucheries. Much of the food, such as bread and pies, was baked on the premises, so the smell mingled continuously with the scent of oil paints and Gauloises.

Every building contained a warren of studios and students displayed their pictures on the pavements. There were no tiresome souvenir shops. In fact the quartier was not really famous in those days and remained what it had been for so long: a living, working area for aspiring artists, who could find a cheap studio, attend the classes of a *maître*, and indulge in endless conversation with like minds.

The whole area is dominated by the Basilique du Sacré-Coeur, and when the conversation at a café about the meaning or philosophy of art became too heavy for me, I would wander off into the Basilique to indulge my preference for solitude and silence. I gained the impression that those who talked the most about art, or anything else for that matter, were those who did the least.

I loved the Sacré-Coeur. The clear controlled lines and open vistas impressed me more than the darker Gothic interiors of medieval churches and cathedrals. The place was restful, and the space allowed my soul to expand. I have always loved observing, and it was mostly the street urchins and the Sisters of Charity that caught my eye in the Basilique. The street urchins came in to escape the cold outside. Ill-clothed, wearing boots with the toes cut out to allow for growth, they were dirty, and often pinched and hungry-looking. But also resourceful, streetwise, self-confident. The divide between rich and poor in Paris was great and the poor were very poor, even though a social welfare system had been in existence in France for some decades. Presumably these little urchins had to go to school, but where they lived, what they ate, how they kept warm in winter was a mystery to me. They were not beggars or thieves necessarily, just children of the very poorest class who had to live by their wits. I have seen a crowd of such children follow-ing a baker carrying a tray of freshly baked bread on his head. One of them would jolt him, so that some rolls would tumble off, then others would grab them and disappear in seconds. I have seen a tiny hand appear from nowhere and take an apple from a stall – when the shopkeeper turned round there was no one to be seen. I once watched two boys practising a very lucrative trade. One of them purloined empty bottles from the back of a wine merchant's shop; while the other took them into the front, and claimed one sou per bottle. When asked where he had come by so many bottles, the lad burst into tears and said, '*Mon père, il boit*' (my father, he drinks).

The Sisters of Charity floated around the whole of Paris. I couldn't believe my eyes when I first saw what looked rather like a sailing ship, perched high above the heads of the crowd, sailing along the street. Curiosity compelled investigation. It proved not to be a maritime vessel, but the wimple of a nun, pure white, about a yard across, with wings billowing upwards. In order to maintain her balance, the nun had to walk erect, in a stately manner, and only turn her head slowly.

The nuns commanded great respect. Their presence had a magnetic quality. More than once I saw a group of teenage boys behaving very badly in the streets, shouting, swearing, fighting. A Sister of Charity would walk up to them and have a quiet word, her medieval headdress moving with slow grace. The boys would grin at each other, and perhaps kick a stone to show their defiance, but the fighting and shouting would cease. For street control, the nuns were more effective than the police.

The ancient monastic habit, sadly, was discarded in the 1970s, when the Sisters of Charity adopted a simple grey dress. No doubt it is more practical, but much of the colour and eccentricity of French street life has gone with their distinctive habit.

Helga introduced me to many of the great works of art in and around Paris. Monday was a day when entry to all the museums and galleries was free and as we had very little money, this was a great blessing. With Helga and her friends I wandered all over the Louvre. It bewildered me. I was more impressed by the exterior beauty of the building than by the beauties inside. I remember quite clearly, however, that access to the *Mona Lisa* was absolutely free – anyone could wander around it, and touch it. There were very few visitors, and I do not recall a guard. Today, I understand, she is kept behind bulletproof glass, surrounded by armed guards and peered at by hundreds of people, who are allowed two minutes' viewing time, and then herded on.

We went to L'Orangerie. Helga explained that the gallery had been specially redesigned in the 1920s to accommodate Monet's *Water Lilies*. It had been closed all through the war, and had reopened only recently. Strangely enough, these paintings were not regarded as a national treasure by the French in the fifties and many Parisians grumbled that it was a waste of public money.

We went to the small and intimate Musée Bourdelle which had been the home of Antoine Bourdelle, the sculptor, and was still the house of his widow. The house and studio had been made into a public museum. Bourdelle died in 1929 but nothing was open to the public until after the war. The house and the studios were crammed with hundreds of his huge, craggy, powerful statues. I have always loved sculpture more than painting – I like something you can get your hands on, and feel under your fingers – and I was bowled over by the Musée Bourdelle, far more than I had been by the Musée Rodin, which seemed to me, by comparison, far too mannered and polished. There was a primitive passion and urgency about Bourdelle's sculptures, as though his very life depended upon the work he was doing. I remember almost melting with joy at seeing, and touching, about half a dozen busts of Beethoven, the Mother and Child statues, and the poignant yet strong sculptures of the Polish uprising that nearly moved me to tears.

Mme Bourdelle was a very old lady. Pictures of her youth show a great beauty, with flashing dark eyes, but when I met her she had the frail beauty of old age. I bought a little booklet, which she signed. I keep it to this day.

About thirty-five years later, I visited an exhibition of Bourdelle's work in a sculpture park in Wakefield, Yorkshire. It was terribly disappointing. The exhibits were all cast. None were the originals that I had seen so long ago, and the chisel marks, the rough bits, the immediacy, the intimacy, had all been smoothed out in the process.

We went to Chartres. Sometimes the visual impact of a place can render a group of people speechless. We entered the cathedral a crowd of jolly, carefree young people, chattering about this and that. There was something like a collective intake of breath, and nobody spoke or moved or breathed for about sixty seconds. We all reacted in the same way. A spiritual presence overwhelmed us.

Helga took me to an exhibition by Bonnard. The pictures were nearly all domestic scenes: children, a woman washing, cooking, having a bath, or simply looking out of a window. Lovely, simple portraits, and all of his wife. The dates on the pictures showed they had been painted over a span of forty years, yet in all that time she did not change. To the rest of the world she must have altered from a young girl to an ageing woman, but to her husband she never grew old. Enchanting. True love does not alter with time, nor the object of love change with the passage of years.

Student life was rich. L'Alliance was attached to the Sorbonne, and although the humble foreign students were regarded as inferior beings by the lordly undergraduates, we mixed freely at the all-night parties. Student parties today are so noisy that no

8·7·08

Dear Joyce,

Thank you for your lovely letter.
I adore the story about the pedal
falling off the bike, and the man
with a gun!! What a situation!!
We nurses & midwives had to be able
to manage anything, and we did.
What surprises me is that no-one
has written about us before. We
were real adventurers.

Thank you again for writing.
I will keep your letter & treasure it.

Jennifer Worth

Jennifer Worth
as a child

And with her
husband Philip
and her daughters,
Suzannah and
Juliette

Sister Jocelyn (the nun Sister Julienne was based on in the books) with Jennifer's daughter Suzannah

Cynthia, Jennifer's nursing colleague and good friend who appears in all three books

Father Joe Williamson, mentioned in *Call the Midwife* with regard to his work amongst the poor of the East End

Daphne Jones, who worked alongside Father Joe Williamson at his mission. Photo reprinted courtesy of All Saints' Church, Poplar.

Photos from the workhouse described by Syd Bailey – the orphanage children with some of the nurses, and the children on an outing to Rhyl. Photos reprinted courtesy of Syd Bailey.

Sister Jocelyn was a keen artist and she included beautiful sketches on her letters and postcards to Jennifer and her daughters

Jennifer Lee (later Worth)
at a wedding in 1959

one can hear themselves speak. Not so in former times. Parties used to be for drinking, companionship, but above all talking. We talked the night away, discussing art and music, politics and social questions, literature and poetry. We sat in tiny cold rooms, under the slate roofs, drinking red wine from beakers, putting the world to rights. French students have always been political, active, and very passionate in their beliefs, watched and feared by governments. I did not understand the subtlety of the arguments, and could not join in, but I listened, fascinated. Not long after I left Paris, a student uprising occurred, with barricades in the street and the riot police out with water cannons. Across the Channel in London I followed events with great interest, as many of the young people I had known were involved.

At one of these parties I met a young Frenchman who was blind. He was a pianist, and we sat talking about music. He asked if I would like to attend a student concert the same week at his teacher's house. He told me with pride that his teacher was Nadia Boulanger. The name did not mean a thing to me, but I was pleased to accept the invitation. We met at La Trinité and he led me along the Boulevard de Clichy, into an area of Paris I did not know. From the speed and confidence with which he negotiated the streets and crossings I began to think he was not blind. He did not hesitate for a second, but walked fast along the middle of the pavement, chatting all the while. I remarked on this and he laughed, 'If I am going to fall over, I will do so whether I walk slow or fast.'

He stopped at a door in the rue Ballu. We entered the lift. Those exquisite French domestic elevators that look as if they have been there since the time of Napoleon. The flowery wrought-iron tracery looked too delicate and insubstantial to carry any weight and the interior was so tiny that only two people could enter. As the elevator trembled its way upwards, he whispered, 'She hears everything. She forgets nothing. I am nervous.'

The apartment we entered was a salon comprised of two large drawing rooms, the central doors of which had been thrown open. Two grand pianos, an upright, a chamber organ, a harp, and a collection of other small instruments were situated towards one end of the salon. People of all ages were milling around, talking. We sat down and he whispered, 'Some of the greatest musicians of this century have studied in this room.' I thought he was exaggerating. He continued: 'Some of them may be here this afternoon. But I am not worried about them. It is Madame herself whom I fear.' He was massaging his hands to make them supple. 'She is at home every Wednesday afternoon. You will hear everyone here, from children to internationally famous performers and composers.'

I whispered, 'But how can she teach every instrument? It is not possible.'

'She knows everything. Nothing in music is beyond her knowledge. Her speciality, though, is composition and orchestration.'

I really thought he was exaggerating. I was not aware of being in the salon of one of the greatest musical figures of this century, a woman to whom great musicians such as Boulez, Stravinsky, Ravel, Poulenc, Messiaen and Fauré came for instruction.

A tall white-haired lady entered. She looked very intellectual, I thought. Her confidence, and the deferential way everyone spoke to her, made me think she must be the teacher. The concert started, and Madame commented upon every performance, in the manner of a masterclass.

My friend played a Chopin scherzo. I thought it was brilliant, but she was critical. She made him play a section again. 'Lift the hand here; attack there; legato – more legato – build it up slowly, relentlessly.' The second time he played, it was a revelation. Just a few words and the playing was transformed.

I attended many Wednesday afternoons and heard some

great performers and singers, as well as chamber groups and small choirs. Madame was always the same. She appeared to listen to every note, her attention never wavering. '*She hears everything. She forgets nothing.*'

More than anything, one sound evokes for me Paris of the 1950s: the voice of Edith Piaf. More than any paintings or books, more than the language, more even than the smell of Gauloises, a few notes from her songs, heard by chance on the radio, will stop me in my tracks, and it will all come flooding back.

At the student parties, her records were often brought out. Music today is so omnipresent that no one really hears it. But in the fifties, old scratchy 78 rpm records were prized and closely guarded. The gramophone would be wound up, and we would sit listening, hushed, to the astonishing voice and interpretation of Edith Piaf. Every range of emotion was evoked in the raw, sensual use of her voice – aggression and sentimentality, power and poignancy, pleading and heartbreak.

She had started as a street singer in the 1920s, and progressed to international fame, and great wealth. I had to go to one of her performances. I went to a midnight show, and I went alone. Someone should have told me never to go to hear Edith Piaf alone – it will break your heart. It broke mine. Loneliness and longing for a man far away, and the relentless yearning in her voice, were too much for me, and I wept uncontrollably. Even now, just the sound of her voice, and I can hardly contain the tears.

Helga introduced me to the Russian Orthodox Church in rue Darue. The liturgical music of the Russian Metropolitan Choir of Paris had been famous for over a century, and the chants go back nearly a thousand years. The cantor was a Russian bass, whose voice rose in quarter tones, up and up, almost to the tenor register. The melodies from the small choir were utterly new to me, and riveting.

The Orthodox service lasts from about 10 a.m. to 1 p.m., and people come and go all the time. There are no seats and so there is constant movement, and hushed sounds as people greet each other and kiss, or depart. I would enter quietly each Sunday and lean against a pillar near the choir, or sit on the floor, my eyes fixed on the magnificent gold screen from behind which the cantor and the priests would appear. I had not the faintest idea of what was going on, but something stirred within my soul that was not due simply to the music. I attended most Sundays, and all of the Christmas and Easter liturgical services, which occur one week later than those in the rest of the Christian church.

Only one thing distressed me, and that was the beggars in the street approaching the church. I had never seen poverty and human degradation on such a scale, and found it deeply upsetting. There had been no, or at least very few beggars in London, so I was unprepared for the sight of *les clochards*, as the Parisians called them. Little could I have guessed that the streets of London, at the advent of the new millennium, would be home to far more beggars than I had witnessed in Paris in the 1950s.

Les clochards were everywhere. In winter the open grilles, or gratings, in the pavements were fiercely guarded, each one being 'owned' by a *clochard*, usually a woman. I was told this was because the warm air from the Métro rose upwards and escaped via these grilles. The women slept on the iron bars, for the sake of the warmth.

The men mostly slept down by the Seine, and while at no time did I feel threatened or nervous wandering around Paris alone at night, I would not have attempted to go down by the Seine. They gathered mainly under the bridges, and drank the night away. Sometimes one was aware of fierce fighting among them, so I did not venture near.

The meths drinkers were by far the worst, and the most pathetic. Life would be short, and they were utterly beyond help. The worst thing about meths drinkers is that they cannot contain themselves, and the smell of such a man, or woman, is terrible. No shopkeeper would allow a meths drinker into his shop. The smell would linger all day, and drive the customers away.

I recall a naughty incident on the Métro. Frenchmen were very good at touching up a pretty girl. They would rub an appreciative hand over a tempting buttock or thigh. Perhaps they still do, but as I am no longer young, I would not be so favoured. It had happened quite a few times in crowded places, but this time on the Métro, jolting along, hanging on to the strap, the guy really was going too far. The hand was going beyond an appreciative stroke, the Métro was very crowded, and I couldn't move away. I looked down at this fellow, who looked up at me, smiling as his hand slid between my legs. I moved my foot so that my stiletto heel was right over his instep, and then I leaned on it with all my weight. His howl of pain, and leap for safety, upset the balance of half the people in the Métro car!

At a party one night, when the Algerian question was being discussed, all mixed in with Marx and Engels and liberty and workers, a young Dutch boy whispered to me, 'This is getting pretty heavy. Have you seen Les Halles at dawn?'

We slipped out into the night. It was midsummer, and warm. I took off my shoes and walked barefoot. The night air was calm and smelt sweet. It was about 2.30 in the morning and all of Paris lay sleeping. We wandered through the little streets from Montmartre down to the Seine. A few prostitutes were walking around, and one or two came over to us. The Dutch boy grabbed my arm, and whispered, 'Don't leave me!'

I replied, 'Not for anything. I might need your protection!'

We continued to wander through the streets, and every-where the warm smell of yeast and wheat from the bakeries made us hungry. Bakers worked all night to have fresh bread ready for the critical French housewife first thing in the morning. There were hundreds of small *fournils*, or bakehouses, all over Paris at the time, and they supplied the boulangeries in their immediate area, delivery being made by a man with a great wooden tray balanced on his head.

The lorries, or horse-drawn carts, of the *laitiers* came round with their great aluminium churns of milk. Shopkeepers would have left their empty churns on the pavement overnight, which the *laitier* would take, then replace them with full ones. Most milk was sold in that way. Bottled milk was available, but the older tradition of taking your jug to the local shop to be filled was preferred, and more common.

The shopkeepers began opening up around 4.00 a.m. The *marchands* of Paris worked from dawn till night. I had seen many of them closing shop at about 10.00 p.m., even in the middle of winter. And now here they were, yawning, grunting, pulling at their braces, taking down the shutters at 4.00 a.m. The wives and daughters followed, sweeping out the shop, polishing the windows, laying out the goods. The men would bring out a handcart and start plodding off. We saw many of them, all pulling their carts, heading in the same direction.

'They are going to Les Halles, for their day's supplies,' said my guide.

There was very little refrigeration, and virtually no preservatives in those days, so most foods had to be restocked daily. As no working man could afford a car or van, most supplies had to be carried on these wooden handcarts. The iron wheels clattering over the cobbled streets made a continuous sound which increased in volume as we came nearer to Les Halles.

The great wholesale market of Les Halles lay right in the centre of Paris. For centuries it had been the centre of all food trading, and could be likened to Covent Garden, Billingsgate and Smithfield markets all rolled into one.

We arrived at about 4.30 a.m., and trading was in full swing. Produce was laid out on barrows set between the fine wrought-iron columns that supported the arches. The produce had been brought in from outlying areas around Paris by truck, train, horse and cart or handcart, or donkey. These comic little animals with their ribbons and plaits and bells were often so laden that it surprised me they could even walk. All the vendors were in competition with each other, and passions ran high. The buyers, at that time of day, were all retailers or restaurateurs, spending a great deal of money. The language of trading was new to me. I had thought I could understand French, but could barely follow a sentence of the bartering.

Most of the birds and small game were alive, tied to barrows, or huddled in cages. The purchaser would choose a bird, and then the vendor would wring its neck. Huge strings of sausages hung from wires slung between the slender pillars of Les Halles. There was a terrific trade in horsemeat, and I wondered if they bred horses for meat, or if they just killed old ones. It was all very jocular and good-natured. By contrast, the fruit and vegetable markets were savage in their competition. I had noticed this strange anomaly before in England: butchers seemed to exude the milk of human kindness, while greengrocers seemed sour and pinched. You would think it would be the other way round, wouldn't you?

We ate bowls of onion soup with warm fresh bread, steeped in garlic, and white peaches, drinking wine straight from the bottle, standing on the cobbles. The sky glowed red before we saw the sun, and the long shadows of the tall buildings and the multiple chimney pots fell across the pavements. Many cooks and servants came in their aprons and headscarves to buy for Madame, and her all-important kitchen. Poor women, sometimes carrying babies, came to buy for their families or to gather up the cabbage or turnip leaves lying discarded on the ground.

I loved Paris and I knew that Les Halles was another anchor in my heart and that I might want to stay in Paris for always. But my life was soon to take another, unexpected, turn.

Au Revoir Paris

My easy life in the Boulevard Haussmann was too good to last. I was informed abruptly on a Tuesday that the family was going on vacation that Thursday and that my services were no longer required. I had forty-eight hours in which to find another job. A new job was soon found.

Monsieur and Madame C lived in a big, modern house set inside a walled garden that was guarded like a citadel. The eight-foot-high stone walls had broken glass and barbed wire fixed all along the top; the heavy double doors, made of galvanised iron, were bristling with alarm systems, and the house had more alarms and bars at every window. It certainly did not look inviting, and I accepted the job mainly because it involved looking after only one baby. I thought it would be another cushy number, leaving me with plenty of free time. One should never accept a job with such a motive!

The Cs had four other children who were under seven years old. A girl was employed to look after them. Also employed were a cook, a washer woman, a woman to do the housework, and an elegant Spanish boy who acted as butler and valet to Monsieur. They were all resident. In addition a chauffeur/mechanic was in full-time employment, and he lived in a flat over one of the garages. My responsibility was to look after the four-week-old baby, and I was given a suite of two rooms and a bathroom for this purpose. It all seemed very elegant.

At the interview it was agreed that I must have time for my language classes each afternoon. It had not occurred to me to ask about other free time and I ended up with much less than I had bargained for. I had sole responsibility for the baby, apart from the two hours allowed each afternoon for classes. Gone were my evenings in the bistros and cafés, gone were my interesting companions, my wandering and exploring.

Mme C was a ravishing beauty. Exquisite bone structure, pale ivory skin, dark eyes and hair, she was a picture of perfection. She was also tall and slender, with a firm and shapely figure, which was astonishing in view of the fact that she had had five children, the youngest being only four weeks old. Furthermore, she looked about nineteen, although I was told she was in fact twenty-six.

She was conscious of her beauty, and had been a mannequin at the House of Dior. She walked most of the time as though she were on the catwalk, with her eyes fixed on a point in the far distance, a remote expression in her eyes. She dressed with exquisite taste at great expense, and changed her entire outfit several times a day, but I always found her rather aloof and I couldn't fathom her relationship with her husband.

Monsieur was about forty, small, dapper, and had a furious temper. The way he dressed you would think he was the sharpest thing since Beau Brummel and he kept his valet busy most of the day pressing his suits and ties, and polishing his tiny shoes.

Few people in Paris at the time owned a private car, but Monsieur had five! An English Rolls-Royce, an American Chevrolet, a beautiful French Paccard, and two small Renaults to run around in, for himself and his wife. Each morning the chauffeur would take him in the Rolls or the Chevrolet to his place of employment (I never found out what that was) and each evening collect him. The chauffeur, Georges, spent the day washing and polishing the vehicles. He often went out on little drives to 'test the engine'. The women of the house showed endless curiosity about Georges' excursions in an expensive car and never tired of questioning him about what he was testing, and how the performance rated. He merely winked enigmatically and said that the carburettor needed tickling, or the piston was going well that day. The job suited him down to the ground, and he was a happy man.

The high-walled garden could have been beautiful had it not been filled with garages, a maintenance pit and a mechanic's workroom. Whilst I was there a sixth garage was built, and Monsieur proudly brought home a new Italian Ferrari. It was bright red and gleaming with virgin chrome. Most of the cars of the day were in black or sombre colours, so the vibrant red glowed like a firework. Georges held open the doors of the new garage as Monsieur drove in, and then they spent half an hour talking about the car, caressing it and looking lovingly at the engine.

In some ways I should have been happy, but after a time, I found the strained atmosphere in the house wearing. Also, now that my French had improved, I wanted to broaden my experience and began to look for a job in a hospital.

My first choice had been the prestigious American Hospital in Paris. But then I reflected that I had come to Paris to learn more about French culture and language, not American, so I accepted a post in a small hospital on the outskirts of the city. It specialised mainly in gynaecology, for which about one hundred and fifty beds were provided. I accepted a post in the theatre, as I had had a good training in all branches of theatre work: general surgery, gynaecology, orthopaedics, and ENT. I thought it would suit me well, because most operations are carried out in the daytime, and consequently theatre staff have their evenings off. I had planned to stay for several months but in the event it was only five days.

Attitudes have now changed, but in the 1950s the French tended to have a hard, unrelenting attitude towards girls who became pregnant outside marriage. The family life of the French was closely guarded and sacred. Any girl who stepped outside these social expectations was punished by rejection, ostracism and often poverty. Many girls committed suicide. Many abandoned their babies, and the foundling hospitals were always full, finding new babies on their doorstep almost daily. Many girls had to turn to prostitution in order to survive. During my time in Paris it was reported in the newspapers that a young girl had delivered a baby, in the middle of winter, in the shrubbery that fronted the elegant crescent of some particularly expensive apartments. Many people must have heard her cries. Many must have seen, or at least guessed, what was going on. But no one called a doctor or an ambulance, or even the police. They just drew the curtains to shut it all out. Mother and baby died of exposure and haemorrhage.

At first, I enjoyed working in theatre again. It is good to know that one is expert in a highly skilled job. I worked from Monday to Friday, learning, observing, remembering procedures. But then, late on Friday afternoon, as we were clearing up after a routine operation, news came of an emergency admission requiring immediate surgical intervention. I learned that it was a young girl who was pregnant and had jumped off the Eiffel Tower. In her fall, her ankle had caught on one of the metal girders and she had hung upside down for two hours before she was released and brought down. On the way to hospital, labour had started and abortion was imminent.

I shall not go into the details of that evening, but for me it was the end of my love affair with Paris. I witnessed an approach to nursing so very different from my own. I knew I could not stay and that I must return to London.

Happily my last memories of Paris are not of the hospital, but of Helga, to whom I went for comfort and shelter that sad evening. I rang the bell of her pension – I said to the concierge, 'Fraulein Helga, s'il vous plaît, Madame.' She smiled – everyone liked Helga – and let me in.

The ancient, rattling lift took me to the fifth floor, and then a walk of two flights up to the garrets, one of which Helga rented for a modest amount. I must have looked dreadful when I entered, because Helga dropped something and ran to me.

'My dear Jenny, you are ill, sit down, have some wine. I will make coffee. What is it, my dear?'

We sat for a long time talking about suffering, the mystery of it, the mystery of man's inhumanity to man, and man's goodness to man. Helga was older than me, and had been ten when the war started. She had seen suffering on a scale that I, brought up in the English countryside, had never seen. She had experienced fear, homelessness, hunger, hiding, dodging and weaving in order to survive. She could not resolve the conflict in my heart, but that would have been asking too much. Decades later, I am still pondering the mystery of suffering, and the mystery of redemption, and I daresay I will go to my grave with the conflict unresolved.

Helga was practical as well as philosophical. 'You must stay with me here, until you have made arrangements for your return to England,' she said, 'and now you need something to eat.'

Helga's little room was about nine feet by six, and in it she lived and entertained, and cooked delicious meals, all with the most exquisite order. Her kitchen was about the size of a tea tray, set on a tiny cupboard at the foot of the bed. On a single gas jet, no bigger than a coffee cup, she cooked everything. I began to feel relaxed and happier.

That night, and for the next week, I slept on the thin mat by the door of Helga's room, while arrangements were made for my return to England.

On the last night we dined out at a bistro where many artists and writers gathered. We ate and drank well under a June sky, and discussed the Algerian question, artistic integrity as opposed to commercial art, the writer's dilemma, the difficulty of finding a cheap room, left-wing politics, American intervention in the East. In other words, anything and everything. There was a young boy there called Benoît, whom I had not seen before. He was quiet and pleasant, and only joined in the conversation when his opinion was asked. Most of the time he was sketching. Late in the evening a flower-seller came round, going from table to table. He called out to her, 'I have ten sous left, I want a rose. Will that be enough?' She haggled with him.

'I have nothing more,' he said, 'surely that will be enough?' He had very winning eyes, and soon won her over.

A friend said, 'You are a fool, Benoît, that's all the money you have, why are you throwing it away?'

He laughed, 'It is so little that it is no good to me, and I might as well be parted from it as keep it. Besides, I want the rose.'

We were all looking at him, intrigued. He leaned across the table and took my hand and kissed it, and said, 'For an English rose who is leaving tomorrow.' It was the most extravagant and romantic gesture I have ever experienced, and from a complete stranger.

Later that night I counted out the money that I would need to take me to Calais and pay for the ferry. I had about two thousand francs left after deducting expenses. I asked Helga to commission Benoît to paint or draw me a picture, for which he would be paid two thousand francs. About a month later I received a scroll from Helga in which there was a charcoal portrait of me which he had created from the sketches he had been doing at the table that night. I had the portrait framed, and it hangs in my house to this day.

Jennifer Worth

Helga remained very special to Jennifer and theirs was a lifelong friendship. They met rarely but kept in touch with one another by letter and telephone.

26 January 2000

My dear Jennifer,

After our delightful telephone call, let me return to the extract of your new book once again. As I told you, your sensitive and humorous observations – some of them very exciting too – are fascinating to read, and I realize that you are a very gifted writer.

The happenings in Rosa's family rolled up like a movie in front of my eyes.

As far as myself is concerned, I feel quite flattered, and there are details which have completely escaped to my mind.

The painter who offered you the rose and of whom you received your portrait must have been Alain Trioen, called Borris at the time. Meanwhile 60 years old, he still calls me up about five times a year. His painting was more interesting – in my opinion – when he was young. His success remained very limited, but he remained successful concerning women, considering himself calmed up by now, having only one 'Permanente' (supporting his existence I suppose) and a second woman with whom he 'talks the same language' – from a sentimental point of view I suppose. Alain was brought up without parents, changing his welfare-milieus about a dozen times, no wonder that true love remained a foreign word for him. I join a photo and some printings of his. (No need to return.)

Talking about him to my landlord, a very artistic Polish lady, she wanted to meet him. I invited him for supper and he arrived with fifty baccara roses – in Wintertime, where they cost a fortune! I told him how embarrassed I am – one would have been enough – but inviting him a year later he arrived with a bucket full of carnations. I met him about 25 years ago for some hours in Paris where he offered me one of his sculptures. I could write a book about him and our common time!

The blind pianist you talk about must have been Jean Micaut. As far as I remember he was a pupil of the famous Chopin interpret Alfred Cortot. I have met both of them during a youth contest in the Paris Conservatoire, and later on have heard concerts of Micaut, playing the 24 Etudes and Preludes of Chopin. Due to cultivated old friends in Nuremberg I managed a concert for Micaut in Nuremberg. About two or more years ago I saw a portrait about him on the German television. He has a chair at the Conservatoire of Saarbrücken, if I remember correctly, was shown as you describe him, walking like a normal being through the streets. He was blind already in his youth, so one wonders how he could study notes. Well, he is not completely blind, but almost. Fortunately he could marry, after the death of his parents I suppose. His wife is also an artist, a singer if I remember rightly. I saw her first in this programme and since that time I have gone through many unpleasant happenings in hospitals, which have hurt my memory. (No manifestation of cancer any more. I remain under control.)

One thing I never forget when I was on museum tours with you, my Dear, especially in the 'Cluny': the repeated call of the attendants 'Ne touches pas . . .'

As to the absence of bomb sites in Paris I only learned after the war that this was owed to the German General v. Choltitz (buried in Baden-Baden), who refused Hitler's order to destroy Paris shortly before the end of the war. And just yesterday I learned from a programme about Flanders that the beautiful town of Brugge – compared with Venice – also owes its survival to the refusal of a German General, whose name was not mentioned. Maybe they only could refuse because the end of the war was so close. I wish your highly decorated general – I forgot his name – would have refused Churchill's order to destroy the beautiful town of Dresden too!

Meanwhile it is now January 30. I was always interrupted and have now decided to mail this letter in spite of its bad presentation please forgive me! My energy has reduced very much and everything I do takes too much time. I must dress up, being invited out this evening – together with my wonderful friend Eugen.

There are quite a few things I'd like to add to our common experiences in Paris and to your remarkable 'report', but then this letter would never come to an end. Incidentally, I was 12, not 10 when the war started, but this of course is of no importance.

Let's hope that we shall be able to meet in autumn. As you might know, we have a huge 'Festspielhaus' now (which probably ruins our small town), unless constant sponsors will support it. And of course there are many other cultural events in the Casino-Building and in our beautiful little theatre. Too much indeed for this small town and for our money-purse.

One other remark to your experiences in the Métro, which I shared with you. I never found a seat so I had to mix with the standing crowd – I became so disgusted of these sexual attackers that I changed to the bus, though this was more complicated and more expensive, but less crowded.

I must hurry up now, my dear old friend.

Much love to both of you,
Helga

This letter arrived the year of the attack on the World Trade Center in New York:

29 December 2001

My dear Jennifer,

It was a great pleasure to receive your Christmas greetings, accompanied by three very solemn Holy Kings! I am glad to hear that you are well and happy, and of course I share your worries concerning the future of all the children in this world. It seems as if our globe was moved into a 'listing' position. The consequences of these and future terror acts are unforeseeable. We must be grateful for every day which we can live as we presently do.

How wonderful that you find enough time for writing and piano playing. Music and writing are both like a 'massage treatment' for the soul. I wonder what your book is about which will be published in March. How good that you found a cooperative publisher, this is very important indeed. I remember the time when I coordinated the publication of three different books about the famous Casino of Baden-Baden. It was a very exciting experience and after having completed the most representative edition, I did not talk any more neither to the writer nor to the graphic designer. They cooperated so badly that they almost killed me. Also the printer lost his nerves, because the book had to be introduced at the occasion of a Casino jubilee, and in spite of a year of time for its preparation it was not ready in time.

Your handwriting is as harmonious and powerful as ever, dear Jennifer. As to my own, my often trembling hands have spoiled it, therefore I type all my letters. This year I am very late with my Christmas – respectively New Year's correspondence, due to a very bad fall on my face some weeks ago, with concussion, etc., etc. I will not walk quickly in the darkness any more, that's for sure!

The apartment is completely installed now, which took us

131

several months. Everybody adores our architectural arrangements (two doors have been transformed into bookcases, three doors in every room being just too much, even if they have their antique charm). This house is under preservation order.

Unfortunately I have no possibility any more to lodge my friends, there is no guest room. I found a small pension in the neighbourhood where two young friends of mine have recently lodged, which is very cheap in comparison to local price conditions. But I realized that I do not even have the physical strength any more to serve 3 meals a day. I was really exhausted when the dear youngsters left me. It seems that there is no power any more in my tired body. My dear old friend Eugen is worried about this and urges me to stop such engagements. I must obey, as Eugen has done so much for me. He is a wonderful, helpful man.

Much love to you and Philip, and my very best wishes for all of you, including the grandchildren. May it turn out to be a very good and positive New Year for your family.

Helga

Very sadly, as readers of In the Midst of Life *will know, Helga wrote to Jennifer in 2009 saying that, after many years of increasing ill health, and her mind 'drifting away', she had taken the decision to travel to Switzerland, her letter 'taking leave with just a few words'. Jennifer desperately tried to get in contact with Helga but never did find out whether she had gone through with her plan.*

✦

Dear Jennifer Worth,

I have just read, and so enjoyed, *Call the Midwife*. Your experiences so mirror mine in the 1950s when we were in our 20s, even down to unrequited love and making dresses from block patterns.

My experiences were as a nurse midwife with the Frontier Nursing Service in the Appalachian Mountains in Kentucky.

I enclose some descriptions of life in the hills written soon after returning to England. I do hope you might enjoy them.

Yours sincerely,
Anne Rossiter

Anne Rossiter has kindly shared some of her experiences of the Frontier Nursing Service:

It was September 1955 when I set sail on the *Queen Elizabeth*, leaving my boyfriend and England behind for a rather uncertain adventure.

From New York an overnight train took me to Lexington, Kentucky, and then a rickety old bus winded and rattled its way for four hours into the Appalachian Mountains of Kentucky. The hills got steeper and steeper and the country got rougher and rougher till we reached the little town of Hyden. Here was the headquarters of the Frontier Nursing Service and the small hospital. I was met by friendly nurses and lots of dogs.

The FNS was started by Mary Breckenridge in 1925 specifically to care for the mothers and babies of this wild and lovely country. There being no trained midwives in America, she recruited us from England.

After two weeks' training in the philosophy of the FNS, how

to ride a horse and how to drive a jeep, we were sent out to our outpost sited about 12–15 miles from Hyden. There were about seven outposts each with two nurses, two horses, two jeeps and one cow, chickens and dogs.

Our area radiated about seven miles around our centre, which was called Beechfork. Here in Asher there was one made-up road. The mountains were small, wooded and so close together that travel was by horse or jeep, up creeks or along horse trails, up over mountains from one 'holler' to another where the families lived. The people were descendants of settlers who had stayed in the mountains, with names like Smith and Caldwell, who still spoke using words like 'yonder'.

Our main task was to deliver the babies and look after the mothers both before and after birth but we also inoculated the children and did what we could for any medical need. During the day we could 'wind up' the telephone and call the doctor, who could come out for visits or for emergencies.

My two years in America gave me a great love of the country and its people and I made lifelong friends.

Dear Jennifer Worth,

During the 1950s and 60s I worked in the London Docks. I travelled continually to and fro between the Surrey Docks in Rotherhithe, through the tunnel and along Poplar High Street, to Thames Wharf at Canning Town. I often visited the timber yards of Montague Mayer and John Lenanton at Millwall, and I was also involved in the Finnish Seamen's Mission, which was then in Branch Road, Wapping. I got to know Wapping Wall and Cable Street pretty well, though I never had occasion to stop there.

Because I had been familiar with East London, I was prompted to read the book *Call the Midwife*, and I must say it is a damn good read. I have recommended it to a lot of people. It then struck me that the author's name seemed familiar, and after a bit of research, I worked out that it had to be the lady in Box-moor with whom I had already corresponded on the subject of GM crops in 1991.

So I am writing again to say that I really did enjoy your book.

I want to make a few observations on the difficulty of writing *any* dialect of English. The problem is that in English you can't tell how to pronounce any combination of letters out of context. When I was confronted with *'eedin:ough:oo'ave'i:i:* I did not immediately know whether the *ough* should be sounded as in tough, Slough, thought, cough, or Woughton-on-the-Green. However, once I understood the idea, I found I could read and understand the Cockney without reading the English first. So I think it was a pretty good effort on your part!

I think the Cockney speech form of replacing *th* with *f* and *v* is much older than you suggest. John Roque made a map of London around 1790, and he shows a street near Soho Square as *Thrift Street*. However, the maps made after 1800 give it its present name of Frith Street. I suspect it is actually pronounced *Vrith Street*, because had it occurred to you that in the examples you give, the Cockney *f* replaces the unvocalised *th* as in *This-tle*, while the *v* replaces the vocalized *th* as in *This*? The Welsh would write *This* as *Ddis* to show the distinction in sound. No dialect is lazy speech. Grammars differ from one dialect to another, but they all have a grammar. The expressions *This here* and *That there* translate exactly into correct Swedish as *Det her* and *Det dar*, and the Swedes don't see those expressions as being in the least bit vulgar. My father used to use the expression 'He turns round' a great deal, but I never knew it was Cockney. Father came from Shepherd's Bush, but my mother had been to St Paul's Girls' School, and must have beaten any London accent out of Father before I noticed it.

You really have written a good book.

Yours sincerely,
Colin Davies

Colin Davies had been asked to review Call the Midwife *for a local history society. In his review, he summed up some of the appeal of Jennifer's writing:*

The joy of this book is in the descriptions of the East Enders, and the way they lived, and their humour . . . most of the stories are very funny, but there are some sad stories, some appallingly sad stories, and also happy stories. Each story brings something new, and by the time I was halfway through the book, I was starting to wonder what on earth was going to happen next. I kept wondering that, and I was never disappointed when I read on.

Dear Jennifer,

Now I have finished *Call the Midwife* I must tell you how much I admire your very well-written book. It is so cleverly constructed that the stories become more and more absorbing as the book progresses. By the end I felt you had beaten James Herriot at his own game. I kept longing to get back to the book for another instalment.

I was delighted to find (p. 115) a fellow Trollope fan. I'm a great re-reader, and was on a rerun through the six Barsetshire novels and the six politicals when your book came, almost at the end of *The Eustace Diamonds*. I finished it, then had the joy of your immensely readable book.

Warmest congratulations on your fine and moving book, and very best wishes for it and you. Kind regards to your husband too.

From Fabienne Smith

Jennifer's religious faith was a key factor in her life. In 1958 she decided to write a musical diary, but it quickly became a journal in which she also detailed her struggles not only with her faith, but with the direction she was being called in and her future career. In it she mentions the guidance and strength she found in Sister Jocelyn.

The diary came to light as recently as 2013, giving a fascinating insight into the young Jennifer and also a glimpse of the writing style that was to characterise her books in years to come.

Paris 1958

12.4.58

I really feel it is time I started a musical diary. I have had the idea in my mind for some time but done nothing about it, but if one does not set to work and do what one wants, when one wants, it may never be done.

The idea is for none but my own benefit, to record what I have heard, thereby, to some degree, perpetuating it in my mind: it is so easy to forget sound that passes.

After 3 years of near-sterility in the art that interests me above all, I am beginning, but only just, to pick up the threads again – not that I ever had many threads to drop, that is. Each of the 3 French families with whom I have lived these past 5 months have possessed records, to which I have listened avidly. To learn again to listen was, and still is, the first difficulty – that of course is the great trouble with records, it is all so simple and so cozy, you forget that something great is passing without being heard.

Right now Mme C has a small collection of lovely records of which I have use. Firstly, a name to remember, not known to me before, that shows you how ignorant I am. Zino Francescatti. A glorious violinist, even I who know nothing of the violin can hear that. A concerto of Tchaikovsky in D majeur and particularly the lovely concerto in E minor, Op. 64 of Mendelssohn, again hardly known to me! Peace, calm, joyful optimism, a sense of well-being – wasn't Mendelssohn called the happy composer, with an ideal family life and a loving wife? I must find that out. The orchestra is the New York Philharmonic, conductor Dimitri Mitropoulos. I must make a point of observing and noting foreign conductors of whom I know nothing.

The record that has excited me more than anything I remember is that of Beethoven's 3rd concerto in Ut mineur. Pianist Emile Gilels. Again a complete stranger to me, but if I have any fine sense of hearing, if I know just a little about the piano, I would observe that this Russian is one of the finest pianists I have ever heard. His technique is astounding. I do not know the 3rd to make any comparison, but his interpretation seems to me perfect. Perhaps this is just my first fine careless rapture, and I have mistaken a second rater for a first rater – I have no idea but I must try to find a reputable opinion on the subject of Gilels. Anyway I am so impressed by him that when I get my pay, I intend trying everywhere to obtain the same record, even though I have no gramophone, and no likelihood of possessing one and it will probably cost me 2,000F (or more!).

Next, particularly lovely, Beethoven's 9th sonata for violin and piano in la majeur. David Oistrakh playing (a familiar name to save my self-respect) but I did not know intimately the sonata. Lovely, lovely shining music, the adagio, the variations, the finale presto, each a small treasure house. The sort of music you could hear all your life, and never grow tired of it.

One or two other short entries appear, simply giving details of composers and pieces. Finally, she writes:

21.4.58

Do I ever have any luck? I leave Paris on the 28th and on the 2nd May Francescatti is playing, then again on the 6th.

The diary then jumps to 1959 when Jennifer is back in England. She is staying with the Nursing Sisters of St John the Divine (NSSJD), studying for her Part 2 midwifery.

Easter with NSSJD

24 March 1959

Yesterday I was so joyful about religion: so clear, so obvious, so easy. Today – just the opposite. Yesterday, so confident. Today, full of doubts. Just carry on, that is all for it. Pray for faith, pray for perseverance – no more. Expect only a pushing off from others – the rest is up to oneself.

25 March – Holy Wednesday

Pray and not to faint. Christ had to pray ceaselessly and in just the same manner as we. Through prayer the will of the Father is known; that men should love one another. I have started on the road, and shall have to pass through fire, but there must be no turning back. Let me keep a vision of perfection ahead of me.

26 March – Maundy Thursday

Let me not forget this day in which the certainty that God exists reigns. That this is His kingdom and that we are here to do His will. This time of thought and prayer is a preparation for me. 'To whom much is given, much will be required.' The Watch all day and night.

27 March – Good Friday

Do not seek conflict from Christ – you will not get it. Seek rather service and activity. Evidently all was divinely created, including man, and all is perfection and harmony, excepting man. If mankind is to take his proper place within creation, he must be reunited to the divinity – and therein lies the difficulty – a life's work. All must be rendered up eventually – piece by piece.

28 March

It is so clear – God is all – what is outside him is not. God is love, and God is laughter, light, joy – everything. I have been so greatly blessed by the *conviction* that God is ever-present, all-controlling. Nothing can seriously go wrong. A day such as this, filled with little visions, must be charity, indulgence to my blindness, so that when darker days come I may recall that I have seen a veiled fraction of the glory that is God. This is knowledge indeed!

Easter Sunday

There will be no turning back now: the die is cast, inevitably and irretrievably. It is not a question of choosing – there is no choice, the decision has been made elsewhere. The lake underground has already burst out of a hillside spring which will carry on gathering speed.

In Call the Midwife *Jennifer refers to a broken shoulder, which prevented her from taking her Part 2 midwifery exams.*

31 March

Thank God I broke my shoulder. It was, quite literally, a work of God. As though a hand was placed with such compelling strength on my shoulder that it broke under the weight, and a voice said, 'Stop in this headlong flight of yours and think.'

I did not think – I have done enough of that with too little profit – I fell down on my knees and prayed. From whence cometh all light and life, all strength and hope.

Lord am I happy! Ecstatically! The Lord of life is love, no more. I love, not that I may be loved, but because I must love. It is the original creative force. There is no life but in God. All things come from and return to God. And I am part of that life, my God! Let me record this time of ecstasy, lest I forget thy face when darker days shall come, oh Lord.

Jennifer went to the Community of the Presentation in Folkestone, a nursing community, which took people for convalescence.

2 April, at Folkestone

The Lord will admit no vanity or self-deceit. Let me be humble, let me be pure in heart and sincere. This is a time for thought, for prayer and self-examination so that I might emerge stronger and cleaner, ready to start the work of living as the Lord would have me live.

One is asked to do no more than to follow humbly the way of Christ, with faith and love.

4 April

My thoughts have led me this far; I believe utterly in God, creator of all things and loving protector of all things. This must have consequence for the whole of life. At present I can do only one thing – abandon and break up my old self and habits, and start again in a more Godly fashion. I must obey Sister Jocelyn and the Rector in everything, and this will be my beginning. (This, that I can *do* is a bit hazy. I must think more of it later.)

Over Holy week I was shaken to my rather shaky foundations. As clear as daylight shone for me the eternal truth that there is but one God, the almighty creator, the only reality and that Christ is the son of God. I have never been so shaken. As though it were written in great letters across the sky I can see that there is no life outside God.

For almost a week I was quite literally not responsible for my own actions. My mind and my soul was in a turmoil. I had to get away this week, be alone in order to think. I feel calmer now. Hours of solitary pondering have made me see just as clearly that a revelation is only the beginning.

How did all this come about? First through prayer for light, then through logical thought (even feminine logic!). The Rector taught me to pray, and knowing my blindness I prayed for light. I received it like a glass of cold water being thrown in my face! I was left spluttering and feeling rather foolish. I had to get away to nurse a far greater break than my shoulder. Prayer and thought have shown me that there is only one possibility – to follow the way of Christ, who said, 'I am the way, the truth and the life. No man cometh to the Father but by me.' I know nothing. I must go right to the bottom in order to learn.

How is it that I have come to all this at 23? Most people are 53, if at all, before they realize that the works of the world are empty nothingness if separated from God.

7 April

Letter to Sister Jocelyn:

'I thank God that I was able to come here, and that I was given time in which to think upon the shock that I received over Holy Week.

It is clear now what I must do – place myself in complete submission to you and the Rector until I can stand alone. I must be unmade. I know nothing and must begin at the beginning.'

Went to Canterbury. I prayed hard for love, for I do not seem to love God as I should. Something said to me 'all in God's time. Don't expect a grand passion overnight. You could not have coped. Love will develop and the hand of God guides. Be rather, faithful.'

9 April

There is nothing outside God. Life without Him is thus emptiness. Knowledge, which is not knowledge of God is idle chatter and mistake. At the base of everything is God; a glimpse of this truth, such as I have had, will found the faith of a lifetime, I must remain constant to this conviction, pray for purification that I may be a servant of God, and in the meantime wait, work quietly, and watch until my time is ready. I must be emptied in order that the Grace of God can find room to enter. May God guide me and may I be aware of this guidance.

Prayer:

During Holy week I prayed for light, and received it with a blinding impact. Then I prayed for guidance once I was alone. The answer came – 'follow me'. Now I pray that I may be made worthy to be a servant of God. Today I saw that this is not enough, that I must endeavour to remedy some particular defects in my character, the which I think must be lack of discipline but I am not altogether sure – another sin may be at the root of my defects. In any case, from now on I must get up an hour before breakfast each day, for thought and prayer, and make it into a habit.

22 April

It is easy to sit and read devotional works, nod your head in assent, and imagine you are doing yourself good thereby. In reality you are merely brushing across the surface of your mind, leaving the depths untouched. Filling in time, to one's own self-satisfaction!

I was given a limited mind to understand these things. But my capacity for loving and self-giving is limitless! To think upon and practise an endless love for God and His creation will lead me by a straight road to the Kingdom of God, which understanding cannot even attain to.

25 April 1959

Much grace has been granted to me of late, and I am apprehensive of losing it, lest I should fall back into my empty ways, imagining that that is how I was meant to be, and this Easter grace an illusion.

I have benefitted so much, so very much. Light came where there was darkness, peace from struggle, purpose out of chaos. I see clearly, where before I was blind. I can think with calm confidence. I know what I am doing.

All this must (I hope so much) reflect in my behaviour, for Aunty Doris remarked, 'Jennifer has grown into such a nice girl, quite suddenly she has changed. Has a sort of peace about her. Become so sensible.' She did not realize that it was not me, 'growing into' anything, but grace bestowed upon me from without.

What is it, this grace? How have I acquired a part of it? How is it retained? I cannot possibly say what it is, but I know that it exists. It is acquired and retained by utter faith in and reliance upon God, and by prayer. The habit of prayer and thought is the most important. Consciousness of divine grace will pass away, but habits do not. They become part of a character if carried out each day.

Cynthia completed her midwifery ahead of Jennifer and decided to take holy orders; however, she soon gave it up.

Met Cynthia. She has given up her postulancy. I was shocked by the haunted, lost expression in her eyes and voice. Wrote to her trying to say that suffering is a testing, designed to strengthen, purify and enrich – but failed in my letter. I know just what is meant, but the expression of it is near impossible.

One day, I too will have to experience similar blinding disappointment. Suffering is essential to mental and spiritual growth. May I be granted the grace to remember this, and the strength to profit by and overcome whatever adversity may beset me.

28 April

The Lord is all love and graciousness. May the love that has transformed my life be transferred to the creator of love – the beginning, the end, the gracious giver of infinite love.

Sunday, 10 May

A missionary from South Africa preached tonight about the dangers of imperialistic colour discrimination. The world is seething with activity, oppressed races rising against European-type superiority. Only Christian love will be strong enough to meet this force. There is work to be done, work everywhere.

11 May

My prayers tonight told me this: Belief can remove mountains. To doubt the possibility is to doubt the power of God. I must think only on this.

16 May

I prayed for help in attaining towards the kingdom of God – at which I seem so inadequate. Help came in this form: Have faith that you will get there one day. Believe utterly that in God's manner you are daily being helped in your search. Expect disappointments, but never doubt that they are all unseen aid in reaching God's kingdom. And you will get there!

18.5.59

I owe much to the Rector who taught me to pray, for without it there can be no understanding. An incredible thing, unbelievable to those who don't believe in it, but life-giving to those who do. I asked for light and received great blessing. The rector's orders were very simple: 'ask for what you need spiritually, upon your knees admitting your inadequacy. And make it a habit: 30 minutes each night, no less.'

20.5.59

I prayed, 'Oh God give me work to do in thy name.'
'You will have work to do, but first you must be prepared for it. All that happens accept as My preparation.'
Is it literally God who replies to my pleas?

30.5.59

I heard today that they cannot have me at Lambaréné. Any disappointment felt, I quickly put from me, for such matters are not in our hands.

Jennifer reapplied in 1960 and was accepted, but this time turned them down because she felt unable to leave the church.

13.7.59

Before entering Carmel: 'How interesting is this world when one is about to leave it.' *St Teresa de Lisieux.*
Treat everyone and everything as though just before leaving it forever.

147

Great Lord send thy Holy Spirit upon me. For all that has been given to me, I thank thee with all my heart. In time all I will render up, in service and thanksgiving to thee.

The Rector tells me to start a systematic self-examination. I dread starting – it seems the most distasteful job ever contemplated.

18.7.59

Still putting it off – I dread starting in earnest.

21.7.59

It struck me suddenly today that genuine self-examination is a gift of God and can be completely profitable if I am obedient to my own conscience, and render everything before God, seeking His forgiveness and compassionate grace. God comes from everything.

I pray God to reveal to me the *truth*, nothing else. Not what I imagine, or want to see in myself, only the truth. I am helpless – I cannot examine myself – but I can permit God to show me myself as I really am.

25 July 1959

The basis of Christianity is practical day-to-day virtue, upon this a spiritual life can be built, and upon nothing else. First things first – attend to faults and all else will follow after. Deception first.

26.7.59

The Lord has heard my prayer, and has given me hope and encouragement. Sister Jocelyn says that I may stay here on the general side for a time. A time in which to learn, to examine myself, to correct my faults and build a foundation for my life.

Mercy is granted upon mercy. In staying here my soul is being filled with understanding – and yet I know nothing!

The infinite love of God is drawing all things together. Moving the pieces of the jigsaw to fit into a coherent whole.

30.7.59

My pupilship ended today. From tomorrow I must pick myself up and behave as a responsible adult, equal completely to any other lay-sister. With God's grace and help, I can succeed.

4.8.59

I have been terrified of being 'left alone' with faith and no guide – the darkness the saints speak of. Another flash of insight was granted to me: anyone who consciously tries to do God's will, cannot be left alone. This is to live in love and charity with your neighbour, offering everything to God. Just one simple action done for the sake of God, brings Him right to the centre of your life. To do your own will leaves one alone, removed from God and this cannot be bridged by prayer. To try to do God's will, is a living prayer.

19.8.59

In prayer and sacrifice lies our strength.

The diary ends here and was presumably forgotten about for many years. It resumes some eleven years later, when Jennifer was a busy mother of two young daughters.

8.12.70

I showed this diary, about which I had no remembrance to Sister Jocelyn. She sent a sweet note: 'Go on using it. Go on trying to give to God all that you are, for you are His.'

'Oh God who has prepared for those that love thee such good things as pass their understanding. Pour into our hearts such love towards thee that we, loving thee above all things, may obtain thy promise which exceeds all that we can desire.'

It is Advent; the world awaits the coming of Christ with another Christmas – I must await His coming to me.

12.1.71

A spiritual reawakening almost without my knowledge, consent or understanding has occurred. Prayer is inevitable, and central to each day.

Peace and happiness are always with me, and an awareness that much will be expected of me, for which I must be well prepared.

There are no further entries and the diary was tucked away in a bottom drawer, probably untouched and unread until now.

Edited by Suzannah Hart, June 2013

In the late 1950s after completing her midwifery training, Jennifer considered spreading her wings and working abroad. Her enquiries led her into contact with the hospital set up in Lambaréné by Albert Schweitzer, the world-renowned German physician, theologian, philosopher and medical missionary, who had received the 1952 Nobel Peace Prize (which was awarded in 1953).

24 March 1960

Dear Miss Lee,

Here comes good news for you. A South African nurse, who works here as midwife, returns to South Africa at the end of May or early in June. Are you willing to take her place? We are 8 nurses in the hospital, Swiss and Dutch, a group of about 15 natives help us. And we would be very pleased to see you among us. There is no question of a contract; staff members are free to come and go. But Dr Schweitzer always hopes, that doctors and nurses help him for at least 2–2½ years. Then they go on furlough and come back after a rest of some months if they wish to come and help for a second sojourn. Dr Schweitzer pays your trip, he pays the clothing you need, dental care and other necessary expenses.

1. So, if you decide to come, could you write me at once when you could come? Do you think it would be possible to come at the end of May or début Juin?

2. Then go to a *good* dentist. Dr Schweitzer pays the expenses.

3. And go to the French Consulate in London, where you ask for a visa for 3 months. As soon as you were on the Consulate, you write me in a letter, sent by *air-mail*, *when* you were at the Consulate, address of Consulate, if possible the name of the

Consul-General. As soon as you get your visa, you send us a *cable*.

4. You must also go to a photographer, as you will need 2 × 12 photos de passeport here in Lambaréné.

5. You probably should come by plane. There seems to be a direct plane London–Paris–Marseille–Doula–Libreville–Lambaréné. The Albert Schweitzer Hospital Fund will pay your billet.

6. Outfit. When you come by plane, you can only take a limited number of items with you. I would propose, that you take *12 white dresses*, made of strong cotton material, a very simple façon. Don't use any material with nylon or with a silk thread. Just a good strong cotton, easy to wash. Pockets are the best inserted into the seam of the skirt.

On Sundays or other special days you can wear a better dress, but it should also be solid and simple.

Aprons will be made here.

You must buy 12 slips.

Stockings we have here, as well as *underslips*.

Do buy 5 pairs of *shoes*, good solid 'molières', easy to repair. Black or brown. Sandals cannot be used here. For Sundays you may wear a pair of white shoes, if you want. If possible buy shoes that are rather light.

You must buy a *sun-helmet*, as it is difficult in general to find any in Lambaréné. *Not* out of plastic material. Cotton *nightdresses* are here.

Raincoat: a plastic one is very hot. Better buy a 'gabardine' or 'loden'.

Toothbrushes are here, but when you have a special toothpaste, do bring some with you.

Handkerchiefs are here.

If you want to send some personal things by boat, you should pack it in an iron trunk, closed with two padlocks with double key. You write on it, with white or black paint:

Compagnie Maritime des Chargeurs Réunis
Port-Gentil, République Gabon
Afrique Equatoriale

Agency of the Chargeurs Réunis in London is:

Gellatly Hankey and Co. Ltd
Dixon House
Lloyds Avenue
London EC3

The Compagnie Maritime des Chargeurs Réunis is a shipping company with an office also here in the harbour of Port-Gentil.

Once more about your visa

1. You ask for a visa for three months.

2. You tell at the consulate that you wish to go to Lambaréné as a tourist and you give the invitation, is attestation, which Dr Schweitzer sends you herewith.

3. *Do not mention* that you want to help in Lambaréné as a nurse for a period of 2–3 years. For administrative reasons you must say that you wish to travel to Africa as a tourist and that you ask for a visa for the Gabon for 3 months. From here it is very easy to ask for a prolongation of your visa. This is the official way!

Mrs Clare Urquhart is in England at present. Please do contact her for a sum of money to cover your expenses. She will give you the address of one of the members of the committee of the Albert Schweitzer Hospital.

Once again, kind regards,
Miss A. E. Silver

27 March 1960

Chère Miss Lee,

Laissez-moi vous dire combien je suis heureux à l'idée de vous voir à Lambaréné. J'espère que cela sera bientôt.

Avec mes bonnes pensées votre dévoué,
Albert Schweitzer

27 March 1960

[Dear Miss Lee,

Let me say how happy I am at the idea of seeing you here in Lambaréné. I hope it will be soon.

All my best wishes,
Yours truly,
Albert Schweitzer]

Attestation,

Je soussigné Albert Schweitzer, Docteur en médecine, certifie par le present, que mademoiselle Jennifer Lee est invitée par moi à venir comme mon hôte à Lambaréné, pour faire connaissance avec mon hôpital. Le besoin est je me porte garant de son cautionnement.

Monsieur le Gouverneur, Chef du Territoire du Gabon a fait connaître par lettre 1424 du 4 Avril 1931 qu'il dispensait mon hôpital du versement des cautions.

Fait à Lambaréné, le 27 mars 1960.

Très respectueusement,
Albert Schweitzer

[To whom it may concern

I the undersigned Albert Schweitzer, Doctor of Medicine, hereby certify that Miss Jennifer Lee is invited by me to come

154

as my guest to Lambaréné, to see my hospital. I undertake to be the guarantor of her bond. The Governor of Gabon stated in his letter 1424 of 4 April 1931 that he exempted my hospital from paying bonds.

Lambaréné – 27 March 1960.

Yours respectfully,
Albert Schweitzer]

In the end, Jennifer felt called to remain closer to home, with her own church and through her nursing duties in the UK.

3 Mai 1960

Dear Miss Jennifer Lee,

Of course we do regret that you feel you cannot come. But we respect your feelings, that you don't wish to be outside the care of your church.

Dr Schweitzer sends you his best wishes and kindest regards. And so do I.

Yours sincerely,
(Miss) Ali Silver (Dutch nurse)

Dear Mrs Worth,

My eldest daughter gave to my wife a copy of your book *Call the Midwife*. My wife, who was a Theatre Sister at Guy's when we met and married in 1962, was most impressed and urged me to read it as well. This I have done and I'm bound to say that it is one of the most memorable books I have ever read. I am a retired solicitor, so have little knowledge of medicine except what I have acquired over the years as a part-time Tribunal Judge.

Your experience in the East End was so well told in the book which my wife and I found at times so tragic, at times hilarious and always of interest.

Over the years we met, from time to time, Daphne Jones, whose family used to own what became the Convent School at Lechlade which my two daughters attended, and her sister came to live in Fairford just round the corner from us. I am enclosing a tribute and record of her Memorial Service for you.

Your book reminded me of times in Swindon (15 miles away where I practised for 35 years) and I represented large numbers of folk who were dispossessed of their houses under a scheme very much like you mention at p. 5. At p. 10 you state that nurses were able to walk alone safely at night; my wife had a flat in the middle of Bermondsey and had the same experience. I well recall taking what we called 'NSPCC children' for a picnic and games in Savernake Forest and being told by many of them that they had not seen a cow before although there are farms all round Swindon – and didn't the children smell, just like so many of your families! Another memory – stoves in Barracks were just like you mention – OK if you were near them but cold just a few feet away. I remember when *Lady Chatterley* was published. I was then an articled clerk and joined the huge queue to buy a copy – very disappointing too. One final memory: when I was doing National Service I was very amused to be told (in a squad doing drill) that 'we were like a fart in a colander'. We then went on our first weekend's leave and spent the night on the train from Liverpool Street to Catterick and we were just in time for Parade. We looked dreadful and drilled worse. The same Sergeant, with a twinkle in his eye, then said, 'This morning, you really are like farts in a colander.' I think it was at that moment that I realised that Sergeants had a sense of humour and life was not so ghastly as I had thought. At p. 210 you report the same expression which I last heard many many years ago.

Altogether a wonderful book and you are to be congratulated. Please sign my enclosed book plate.

Kind regards,
Sincerely,
Graham Young

✦

4 July 2005

Dear Mrs Worth,

I have just finished reading *Shadows of the Workhouse*, which I bought at The Mustard Seed, having read *Call the Midwife*, which you signed for me.

I just could not put the book down, I enjoyed it so much. Well, perhaps 'ENJOY' is not always the word, I found it very moving, especially about the child abuse, and about the old soldier. Although I have lived in Hemel for 16 years, my family came from inner London. My father was one of 14 children, and I have heard many stories from him. His mother and sisters worked in hand laundries for a pittance, he and his brothers left school at a very early age and worked with horses, before joining the Army on false ages. Both his father and his elder brother served in WW1, his brother William saw the angel at Mons. (My uncle told me this many times, and said, 'Do not believe anyone who says it did not happen.') My great-great-grandfather was 'Chennells the grocer' in Hemel High Street, who later became Mayor in 1901. 'Our' side of the family came to London looking for work. They never found much of it, and were always poor, but always happy, with a great sense of family cohesion. So your book was very real to me.

Best wishes, and thank you for writing such a wonderful book!

Yours sincerely,
Denise Chennells

Denise Chennells explains in a footnote to this letter:

My uncle, William Pickering, was a sergeant in the Middlesex Regiment. Like many 'old soldiers', he was convinced he had seen the Angel, dressed in white, as the soldiers retreated from Mons. Press reports at the time may have played this down, so as not to seem to be reporting the massive defeat of the British Expeditionary Force. I believe Uncle Willie!

✦

Dear Mrs Worth,

I have only just read *Call the Midwife*, first published in 2002, but I hope it is not too late to thank you for the pleasure it has given.

From 1955–58, I was employed by the LCC Children's Department as a Child Care Officer. My patch was Poplar and Bow, so I worked in Limehouse and the Isle of Dogs and might have passed you in the street.

Your book describes the people, the surroundings and the housing conditions exactly as I remember them.

On one occasion I had to go to a mother and baby home to pick up a child who was being taken into care. I travelled on the Underground with this little black baby in my arms, and got some very odd looks from my fellow passengers. I also remember visiting two little girls, victims of neglect, whose teachers had seen them eating the food put out for the birds at school, and who in consequence were known to us as 'The Breadcrumbs'.

I can remember visiting prostitutes in their homes on more than one occasion, though as I was incredibly innocent it only dawned on me later. I did, however, draw the line at shaking hands with a slimy little Maltese whom I was obliged to visit in Wormwood Scrubs because he had been living on immoral earnings. We, too, found it amusing that the police went about in pairs but we didn't – even in Cable Street.

I never witnessed a birth at that time, but came across the custom of keeping a dead body at home before the funeral. I once unsuspectingly called at a house where a death had taken place. "E's in the front room – would you like to come an' *see* 'im, Miss?' There was the open coffin on a table in the front room, with the corpse looking out of it.

Again, thank you for writing a book which brought back so many memories of a place which I now hardly recognise when I travel through it.

With all good wishes,
Yours sincerely,
Ruth Manley

In her reply Jennifer said:

Thank you so much for writing to me in such detail about time in Poplar & Bow & the Isle of Dogs. I will treasure your letter, saying how accurate my descriptions are. We were in Poplar at the same time so we may have passed each other – maybe you knew about the nuns? You would certainly have heard of Father Joe. I was very interested in your tale about the coffin & the corpse in the front room, and being invited 'to see 'im, Miss'. I've seen this too.

Dear Jennifer Worth,

I felt I must write to you after reading your fascinating book *Call the Midwife* which my cousin gave me last week. I couldn't put it down till I had finished!

I did my Part II midwifery at Forest Gate Hospital, East London, in the early 1960s so recognised areas that you described. Things were much improved in living standards by then – a lot of East Enders had been moved out to the 'new' Basildon in Essex, which is where I was born and brought up (in the rural area of Pitsea) – completely ruined by the 'new' town, it became just a dormitory with fly-overs and -unders, sadly. However, many people still had pretty basic living conditions compared to today and young mums had a lot to cope with. Husbands on the whole did *not* do domestic work of any kind, and certainly would not want to be at a birth, although I remember one man having just gone to bed after being on night duty, who refused to get out of bed when his wife was in labour and had to be 'removed' when she gave birth!

I well remember the old black bikes we had to use – often at night, and we only had a torch and a small map of where we were going and our equipment on the back. As you said, no one *ever* came near us or threatened us in any way. Our uniform was enough to make them respect us. Sometimes, an ambulance man would stop and say, 'Get in the back, luv, where you going?' I shudder now at what could have gone wrong with a labour, but we had the confidence of youth being all of 22 and having just left our teaching hospitals as SRNs. I had been at University College Hospital and the Matron at Forest Gate had trained there too, many years before, so she was always very pleasant to me! The place was very dilapidated and about to be demolished. We had to boil our instruments in an enamel bucket on the stove! (sounds mediaeval now!). The wards were clean but very scruffy and had hardly any equipment as girls would know now!

My mother was born in 1917 and brought up in Stepney by the docks and used to tell tales of the place, when the ships came in laden with spices, etc. – she said you could smell all the exotic scents. Her dad was foreman for a big brewery and looked after all the horses so had quite a good job with a 'cottage' to live in, and only had 3 children, as he came from a family of 14 and left school at 12 to help his mum when his dad died. He said he would never have a big family! But Mum remembered families that were huge and *very* poor – no shoes for kids to go to school and very dirty clothes to wear. The teachers (all ladies) would send my mum out to buy some shoes for them.

If there was a handicapped baby it was hidden away, maybe 'got rid of', certainly never seen. My grandma used to try to help as much as she could with some food or medicines if a child was ill. No NHS in the 1920s! My mum loved it there and when her mum bought a little bungalow in Pitsea, Essex, she didn't want to leave the East End. However, the war came and they left the area forever. I do regret not going back there with her before she died.

We had a *lot* of laughs at Forest Gate (only there for 6 months: two on wards and four on district) and we had an 'older' lady all of 48 (very old) who had come from Rhodesia to do Pt II before becoming a Matron out there. We thought she was *very* old. While there, Rhodesia became independent and she thought she would never get back. I don't know what happened to her.

I am looking forward to your next book about the workhouses. I worked at St Pancras Hospital (part of UCH) in Camden which had been a workhouse previously and many of our 'old' patients were really scared of being there and thought they would never get out.

I was very sad reading about the old lady in your book who was put in a workhouse with all her children and they all died! Life was *very* tough in those days (not that long ago). Imagine that happening now. I sat and cried – you described it all in such detail.

I'm sure you must have kept a diary in order to remember everything. That is my one regret about all my early nursing years, that I did not. I thought I would be young forever and nothing would change but *we* were in the last stage of the old 'Nursing Order' that has now gone forever, sadly – patients looked after properly and not rushed out of hospital.

I do attend the Florence Nightingale Service at Westminster Abbey every year with many other nurses. It's a very moving service – have you ever been? I look back on those years as such happy ones – we worked hard but had fun.

I look forward to reading your next book.

Very best wishes,
Brenda Warwick

Dear Mrs Worth,

I know I'm being very cheeky asking you to sign my tatty but much cherished copy of *Call the Midwife*. It all came about when my son noticed the book on the shelf and mentioned that his girlfriend had a signed copy. I set about trying to convince her to swap copies but she was having none of it!

It transpires that my son went to school with your granddaughter.

I read your book as I was going through the application process for entry onto the midwifery programme at the University of Hertfordshire and it certainly inspired me and spurred me on. Thankfully, I was successful and will be starting my own midwifery journey on the 28th! I do wonder how I will cope with the more difficult aspects of the profession having been moved to tears on numerous occasions whilst reading your story. I think Mrs Jenkins' life story particularly made an impact. I was aware of the old workhouses, of course, but the unimaginable cruelty of separating a mother from her young children in the way you described just had me sobbing uncontrollably! That doesn't bode well for me dealing with the harsh realities of midwifery, does it? But it certainly shows how powerful the written word can be and how you brought these characters back to life in my mind and, no doubt, in the minds of everyone who reads them.

I'm privileged to have the opportunity to thank you (almost) personally for sharing your fascinating experiences and immortalising a little snapshot of our recent history. I look forward to reading your other books – I'd better get the tissues ready!

Thank you for taking the time to read my letter and, in advance, for signing my book.

You are a legend amongst student midwives.

Kindest regards,
Maddy Reid

Jennifer remarked on the importance of the midwife's job in her reply:

I loved reading your letter and so did my husband. It is a happiness to me to know that I have inspired you, and hopefully other midwives also. Remember, when you feel down, that it is one of the most important jobs in the world . . . I gave a talk to the Bedfordshire School of Midwives last year, and it was wonderful to see 150 young, eager faces. The profession is changing, but at core it remains the same.

✦

Dear Mrs Worth,

A friend gave me a copy of your book *Call the Midwife* knowing that I also was a midwife in the East End of London. She did not actually know just how close were our experiences.

I did my Part II training with the Nursing Sisters of St John in Poplar. We lived in Lodore Street, Poplar, at the convent (their mother house in those days was at Hastings but they had two houses: Poplar and Deptford, doing both midwifery and general district work). I was with them from December 1952 to June '53 doing Part II and then stayed on doing a couple of months general district. We covered Poplar and the Isle of Dogs.

You mention in your book Fr Joe – if I remember correctly he was at Wapping. You also mention Daphne Jones – I knew her through the Guild of St Barnabas for nurses. My church, whilst in Poplar, was All Saints'. I arrived in Poplar just after a good friend of mine – a Tommy's nurse – had just married the senior curate – a Mark Hodson, the rector was distinctly suspicious of what he looked upon as potentially predatory nurses!

It was quite an experience working with nursing nuns, wasn't it? Sister Margaret Faith, who was in charge of the house in 1953, died only just over a year ago – a lovely person and such a good nurse/midwife.

After leaving Poplar I returned to the Westminster, where I did my general training, and in '54 became a ward sister there. When I married in '56, I retired – no married nurses then! In fact, my consultant did make moves with matron to see if she would consider me returning after a month or so. However, there was a honeymoon baby en route by then so that plan came to nothing.

My husband was an Anglican priest and we had four children quite quickly after marrying so I was soon fully occupied again!

Yours sincerely,
Jean Todd

✦

Dear Mrs Worth,

I would like to tell you how *very very* much I have enjoyed your book, *Call the Midwife*.

I don't 'go' for present-day novels, preferring to read again and again, my John Buchans, Nevil Shutes, Margery Alling-hams and Georgette Heyers, plus my several non-fiction nursing works, mostly about the war. I was therefore delighted to read the review of your book.

I myself was a nanny all my working life. Not, I hasten to say, with the present day interpretation of the word 'nanny' but of the old days when a nanny's job was 24 hours a day, not the present 9 a.m.–5 p.m. and every weekend off as seems the 'norm' today. And we old nannies dearly loved our charges, a love which was mostly(!) reciprocated by the children.

But my sister, some 8 years older than me, did become a hospital nurse. She spent 1 or 2 years at the London Fever Hospital and then chose to do her general training at Poplar Hospital.

According to my mother, because 'being by the docks, there will be such wonderful accident cases'.

Most probably so – and this stood her in good stead, since she became state-registered in 1938 or 9, joined the QAs, became a nursing sister, and was immediately sent out to France.

After Dunkirk she served at a hospital in Shrewsbury and later followed the army to Belgium.

She will so appreciate your descriptions of the dockland areas and will know much of where you speak. All very differ-ent now, no doubt.

My spirit blanches at the very thought of what you saw and put up with – I am quite certain I would never have done it, even when young. And I have the greatest admiration for you that *you* could and did.

Oh, I will read your book again and again. I loved it all, and as with James Herriot, for the human stories you have also woven into your tale.

Thank you.

Yours very sincerely,
Honor Gray (Miss)

Dear Mrs Worth,

Call the Midwife – A True Story of the East End in the 1950s

I am writing to tell you how much I am enjoying your book, although I have not yet finished it. In view of the subject, I felt I had to write, as it rang so many bells for me.

I am by birth 'an East Ender', having been born in St Andrew's Hospital, Bromley-by-Bow, in 1935. The fourth generation of my father's family to be born in Poplar; whereas my mother came from Hampshire/Berkshire farming stock.

Reading that you were trained as a district midwife by the Nursing Nuns of the fictitious St Raymond Nonnatus, I wondered if this community could be based on the Nursing Sisters of St John the Divine, at Lodore Street (I think), across the East India Dock Road from All Saints' Church?

If so, my late mother, Mrs Lilian Fittock, worked for them as cook from 1947–1952. She was also responsible for cleaning areas of the chapel floor, using a special polish made from Shellac and methylated spirits. The other lady cleaner was a very short lady, Mrs Wade – widow of a policeman.

My younger sister and I sometimes called in on her at work. I still remember the names of some of the sisters. The one in charge was Sister Margaret Faith, together with Sister Jessica, Sister Jocelyn and one with a bad limp (Monica?). There was also a very old Sister Ellen – who wore a gray habit. It turned out she had been a midwife in the 1900s and had delivered my father and his siblings.

There was also their mother house at Sydenham, where 'Sister Nancy' ruled the roost, and they ran a convalescent home at Hastings. When Sister Margaret Faith discovered that my parents enjoyed gardening, but living in an upstairs flat lacked the opportunity to carry out this hobby, they were invited to come to the mother house to clear up the garden, every Saturday during the Spring and Summer. It was heaven for my sister and me because the garden was huge with trees and shrubs. The sisters had a little dog called Brownie who also looked forward to our weekly visits.

The family link with your book doesn't end with the Sisters. Later you write the story of Mary, in the red light area around Cable Street, mentioning St Paul's C.E. School in Wellclose Square. I went into teaching, and my second teaching post 1961–1965 was at this very school.

This was during the time that Father Joe (Williamson) was trying to draw attention to the problems of the area. His two staunch and tireless helpers were Miss Norah Neale and Miss Daphne Jones, godmother and wonderful friend of our particular family. I always wore a loose mac covering me from neck to calves during the time I worked in the area, as it was so threatening to pass cafés with leering customers.

Thank you for writing the book – it opens doors to another world, but you get across the humour, resilience and hard work of those old East End families.

Yours sincerely,
Rosemary Fittock

✦

31 May 2003

Dear Mrs Worth,

I am writing to you to say how very much I have enjoyed reading your book *Call the Midwife*. It brought back to me many memories of incidences I had known, such as you experienced as a pupil midwife in the East End of London in the early 1950s, as I too, like you, am a retired SRN and SCM. I did all my nursing training in the East End, first of all my General Training at the Mildmay Mission Hospital in Shoreditch from 1945–1948 and then my Midwifery Training at the Salvation Army Mothers' Hospital in Clapton, E5 from 1949–1950. The first 6 months of training was spent in the Mothers' Hospital itself and for our second 6 months we were allocated to one of the six different Districts in the surrounding areas of the East End. I spent most of my District Training in the Hackney and Bethnal Green area and lived in a large Victorian house in Hackney Road with 5 other pupils, two staff midwives and the Sister in charge who was also a Salvation Army Officer, as were all the Ward Sisters in the Mothers' Hospital. I thoroughly enjoyed my time on the District and like you we were called out on our bicycles many times during the night to attend deliveries in Shanly and Dack Buildings set in dreadful narrow streets where we were glad to be wearing our nurse's uniforms which we knew would protect us from any undue assault as we penetrated the dark alleyways of the East End. I was very pleased that I was able to learn to practise midwifery under such circumstances and to see how the poor unprivileged people living there coped with their daily living. It was an eye-opener for me, and I'm glad I was able to see life in the raw, as it were, and be of some help and use to those poor mothers being delivered in such difficult situations.

After completing my Midwifery Training and gaining my SCH Certificate, I practised midwifery for 2 years as a staff midwife at Woking Maternity Hospital, Surrey, which was mostly different to the midwifery I had experienced in Hackney and Bethnal Green.

After this I returned to general nursing and eventually became a ward sister, working mainly on women's surgical wards in three different hospitals. The second of these was as a ward sister on the women's ward, Donald Cutrie at Poplar Hospital, where I went in 1957 with a friend and colleague who was a theatre sister and where we were happily employed for 4 years. Being at Poplar Hospital for a considerable time, it was more than interesting to read in your book of your midwifery training in Poplar, as I could picture your experiences there so clearly as we knew Chrisp Street Market and Cable Street. For our last year at Poplar Hospital my friend and I shared a flat in Commercial Road, going to work every morning by bus in company with all the dockers. I was also very pleased to see photos of Father Joe Williamson, whom you knew and wrote about, as I also knew him as he came to speak to us and the Nurses' Christian Fellowship which was held in the hospital on several occasions and we were all very interested as he told us of his Home's work amongst the destitute girls who roamed the Poplar streets. My friend and I were also very pleased to be invited to tea at his Home and meet his co-workers and helpers.

All these coincidences, when through reading your book I feel we share, prompted me to write to you and I wish to express my appreciation and thanks to you for writing about midwives and putting them on the map, as it were, as so many times nurses are written about but not the work of midwives which is so necessary and vital. I am now retired and because of a disability with walking, etc. due to operations on both knees for arthritis followed by 3 subsequent fractures of my ankles, following falls, I am now a resident in a Methodist Home for the Aged, where I have been wonderfully cared for in the past 4 years. One of the senior carers here is hoping to do her Midwifery Training and has been very interested in all I have told her of my past experiences in midwifery. After I had read your book, I offered it to her to read. She returned it to me yesterday saying that she had thoroughly enjoyed it.

So, through writing your experiences you are encouraging the present generation of girls to take up midwifery.

With every good wish,
Yours sincerely,
Ena Robinson

A Modern Midwife
by Sadie Holland

I work as an NHS midwife in South East London, providing caseload care to a group of women – looking after these women before, during and after the births of their babies – just as Jennifer Worth and her colleagues did in Poplar in the 1950s. Six midwives and an assistant work together and we are available 24/7 to about 200 women a year. We come to know our women and their families very well, and although no one *likes* getting out of a warm bed at 3 a.m., it does make a difference when you are going out to a family you know, and when you understand their hopes and fears for the birth – and for the baby. We belong to a large teaching hospital, and many women have their babies there, but because we know our women so well, they often choose to have their babies at home. Some months 30 or 40 per cent of our babies are born at home – rather higher than the national average of 2 per cent.

We have had some marvellous home births. I will never forget one night just before Christmas when the snowflakes began to fall as we arrived; when we left some hours later there was a thick carpet of snow, and not a sound apart from us midwives, hugging each other in the street before setting off home. We helped a publican's baby into the world in a room over the pub, where we could hear lunchtime service going on. One of my colleagues has even attended a birth on a houseboat! I often feel euphoric as I leave a birth, having tucked mother, father and baby up in their own bed – I remember another night singing as I cycled the couple of miles home on midsummer's night, and coming across no people, only 15 foxes. For some women, of course, home birth is not an option, but even for the most high-risk pregnancies, we believe it makes a difference for our women to know their midwife. And I even find myself using techniques learned from *Call the Midwife*. Recently I looked after a tiny baby of only 4lbs, and he spent the first afternoon of his life tucked between his mother's breasts, as warm as toast, licking drops of milk from his father's fingers.

✦

Dear Ms Worth,

It is a complete honour to award your book *Call the Midwife* with a 2009 Mothers Naturally award.

I loved your book, savoured it each time I picked it up to read. Thank you for sharing your story with the midwifery community and the world. The 2009 Mothers Naturally winners will soon be listed on the Mothers Naturally website, the Midwives Alliance website and in the Midwives Alliance newsletter, that will be coming out soon.

Congratulations!

Many blessings to you,
Christy Tashjian, MANA 2nd Up
For all the Midwives Alliance Board Sisters

The Midwives Alliance is a professional membership organisation that promotes excellence in midwifery practice, endorses diversity in educational backgrounds and practice styles, and is dedicated to unifying and strengthening the profession, thereby increasing access to quality health care and improving outcomes for women, babies, families and communities. In 2008, the Midwives Alliance started giving Mothers Naturally awards to authors, activists, blog writers and website creators who exemplify the qualities and values that the Midwives Alliance holds as the gold standard in women- and family-centred care.

(For more information, go to
www.mana.org and www.mothersnaturally.org)

✦

Dear Jennifer,

I was very impressed with your book *Call the Midwife* because of its unusual mixture of earthiness and dignity, the latter quality so often missing from contemporary life. I feel a better person for having read your book and for having shared in the lives of some of your patients who were, on the quiet, exceptional individuals. I could share in the terrible suffering of the likes of Mrs Jenkins and Mary as well as admire Len Warren for having the moral courage to be himself and to admire Ted for choosing life and love instead of resentment and bitterness. You talk about your gradual spiritual awareness with humility and never once did it intrude upon the theme of the book.

I, for one, could do with more books like this.

Thank you.

Sincerely yours,
Pam Hale (Mrs)

✦

8 March 2008

Dear Mrs Worth,

I am writing to say thank you for a brilliant book *Call the Midwife*. I saw it by chance, the title and cover photograph immediately caught my eye. The book brought back so many memories.

I was a staff midwife, later sister at Plaistow Maternity Hospital, Howards Road, E13 in the '60s.

I note you were Night Sister at EGA and was wondering when? I trained at EGA 1958–61 then staff nurse 1961–62.

Having done part of my training at the Dreadnought, Greenwich and the Albert Dock Hospital, E16, I know the area covered in the book well.

I am eagerly awaiting the publication of *Shadows of the Workhouse*.

Again, many thanks for such an enjoyable read and evoking so many memories.

Yours sincerely,
Jean Tomkiss (née Wilson)

Jennifer quickly wrote back:

It was a thrill to get your letter and to know that you loved *Call the Midwife*. Especially though to know that you were at the EGA [Elizabeth Garrett Anderson] – what a lovely hospital! We must have overlapped but I regret I can't remember a Jean Wilson. Do you remember me – either Lee or Worth? I was there from about 61–64. It was a lovely time. I was under Matron Nancy Palmer – a really great lady, and saintly I always felt.

Jean Tomkiss says:

Further to my letter and Jennifer's reply, I sent her the EGA prize-giving photograph for my year. Next day Jennifer telephoned me, delighted to have a photo of Matron Palmer for her collection. She told me that one night at EGA reporters arrived to try to see a patient. There followed great difficulty in getting them to leave. Jennifer woke Matron Palmer who dressed in full uniform and came down to speak to them. Next thing they were seen running down the Euston Road.

The Albert Dock hospital was in Alnwick Road, London E16, at the end of a road of terraced houses. It was part of the Hospital for Seamen. The cover of the *Call the Midwife* hardback caught my eye as it reminded me of the ward office that looked out onto the berth used by Blue Star Line ships with their enormous funnels floodlit against the night sky. It was mainly an orthopaedic hospital taking patients who were seamen of many nationalities and any injured dock workers.

During my time at the Albert Dock hospital, and Plaistow Maternity hospital, E13, one could walk alone about the area and never be molested. A nurse was untouchable. One night on return from leave at Plaistow station an unknown man offered to carry my case. I was a bit perturbed but he said, 'You delivered my baby, my wife would never forgive me if it got about I did not carry your case.'

One New Year's Day, just after midnight, the first baby of the year arrived very suddenly on the ward. Later it was noted the baby appeared very dark but the mother fair. Fearing illness, I enquired if the father was coloured or Asian. The reply: 'Don't know, nurse, it was dark.'

My favourite funny memory was of Antenatal Clinic as a staff midwife. Sister asked me to examine a patient for my opinion. Suspecting nothing I entered the cubicle where a pupil midwife stood, very straight-faced. I removed the covers to see one breast tattooed as a beer bottle 'mild' and the other similar but 'bitter'. Forty-five years later I still do not know how I kept a straight face and carried on!

1 November 2008

Dear Jennifer Worth,

I have just finished reading your amazing book *Call the Mid-wife*, a copy of which you so kindly signed for me at the request of Caroline (Orde) Slack. Thank you so very much. I am still somewhat steeped in the mercifully bygone world you take us back to.

Surely, your book is above all a timely record of Britain's extraordinary recent attitude to the lower class! I can hardly believe it is true and yet I know it must be! We superior British are always so pleased with ourselves! It will do us good to be shaken out of our smug complacency.

My two sisters and I were born to British parents in the Argentine and were all sent to boarding school in England. When I returned to Buenos Aires in 1930 I entered the British Hospital into the Nurse Training School, a fair-sized General Hospital, but no children or midwifery! I had a very interesting year in London in the late thirties – a bit before your time – I worked as a Staff Nurse at the Royal National Orthopaedic Hospital. The place was a shambles. It must have been bankrupt for they were so short of everything! I worked in the children's ward and there were often no sheets, no nappies, almost no nothing for these poor little Cockney kids. The teaching orthopaedic surgeons all worked in the theatre at that time and the incidence of sepsis in the theatres was so high that they had to be closed for a time. I don't know if the Hospital eventually closed down.

I got married at the end of that year and never worked in a British hospital again but it gave me enough to be able to relate a bit to your book. Best of all was your portrait of the Cockney kids and families – amazing people. Your chapter on the

English language 'as she is spoke' was also so fascinating – you could write a whole book about it.

What a hard job it must be – I daresay even today there is a need for more Sister Juliennes.

Thank you.

Sincerely,
Jean Batham

✦

Dear Mrs Worth,

I have just read your book *Call the Midwife* and I am so sad to have come to the end of it. I do hope you *will* write a trilogy as you plan to do and I shall be first in the queue at the bookshop!

I, too, was a district midwife for over 31 years and *so* identify with much that you recount, though my experience was not in the slum areas for the most part. I trained in 1958 and worked here from 1964 to 1995. (I did my training at the Mothers' Hospital belonging to the Salvation Army in Clapton, East London.)

Midwifery was a wonderful profession and I only wish that the young girls training today could know the joy and fulfilment we had. We worked such long hours for very little money but I wouldn't want to be doing the job today. So sad!

Your book is very well written and I enjoyed it enormously.

Sincerely and with all good wishes,
Judy Pemberton

Dear Mrs Worth,

I just wanted to write and say thank you for writing *Call the Midwife*. I absolutely loved it. I finished reading it just 5 minutes ago.

I've just had a baby last September, so can really relate to the book. When I was pregnant with Jessica my grandma would tell me all her labour and pregnancy stories, and I loved that too. Seems women were hardier in the 50s!!

I have to say all the stories made me so emotional as they were so beautifully written. I found myself with a tear in my eye on many an occasion (not great when you're sitting on a bus I must say!!).

Until I had my wee girl, I could not begin to understand how difficult and skilled a job midwifery is. I have such respect for them now, and even more the ones of your generation. How you could do such a job is unbelievable. Reading about Mary was so sad, and Mrs Warren's premature baby story was unbelievable, twenty-five children? I'm still getting used to one!!!, and the premature baby was truly a touching story.

I thoroughly enjoyed reading all the stories, and didn't want it to end. I just wanted to write and let you know.

Yours sincerely,
Emma Hall

Emma Hall recalls of her grandmother:

My Grandma had four kids in the 50s and 60s. She says it was very different then. Once when she went into labour, she called the midwife, then walked along the street to her friend's house, had a cup of tea and sat with her, chatting until she saw the midwives cycling past the window. She said, 'Right Evelyn, here they are, I had better go.'

She says that it was very different, and that pregnancy and labour didn't seem such an ordeal then as it does now. She once waited in labour at home for my Grandad Jim returning home from work before telling him that the baby was on its way. My most recent child, James, is named after him. All of her daughters were born at home. I have no idea where women found their strength from in those days, and how midwives, then and now, do such an amazing job at one of the most special times in a woman's life.

✦

18 March 2010

Dear Jennifer Worth,

I'm sure you won't remember, but just before Christmas I came out of the Maher bookshop at the Howard Centre in Welwyn Garden City, to find you sitting at one half of a long table just outside the Maher doorway. You were on your own. I had just spent a lot of money in the shop, buying Christmas presents for my family, but something made me stop and look at what you were there for.

Well, I bought your book and not only was I delighted at reading the contents, but I found your notes on the Cockney dialect of particular interest.

In this three-generation household we have a daily dog-walker-and-cleaner who speaks with a Cockney accent. She and I have several times discussed the subject and I showed her your notes. She was so interested that I asked her if she would like to take the book home to read in more detail. She kept it until she read it right through (kept her anxious mind off her impending driving test). Not only that, but she lent it to her best friend who also read it.

In Norway, I have a cousin of 80 years who spent a year in the East End of London as a midwife! So I'll send her the book to see if she recognises any of the photos. And she'll probably read the whole book, for her English is good.

I look forward to the next two books of your trilogy.

All the best,
Sincerely,
Joy Wilkins

Jennifer wrote:

I was thrilled with your letter. It gives me great joy to know that people like the stories of the nuns and the district work . . . I am flattered that a Cockney lady approved the book!

Joy Wilkins adds:

I mentioned my cousin in Norway. She had been trained as a midwife and had some experience. She spent a year in England to improve her facility in the language and took a job at the East End, exactly where *Call the Midwife* occurrences took place. I posted the book to her and to her delight it contained photos of the very same places she knew so well!

Dear Ms Worth,

I have often decided while reading a book that I 'must write to the author'. In many years of reading I have never actually carried out my decision! However, your book *Call the Midwife* has had such an impact on me that I have now carried it out!

I was born in 1950 and was brought up in the area between Commercial Road and Whitechapel, just off Sidney Street. We were part of a close-knit Jewish community. Your book brought back floods of memories to me. You are correct in saying that the East End had a finely tuned class system in the differing gradations of the working class. While we were never in the dire straits of some of the people you describe, I saw them all the time on the streets. My mother's sister lived in Barking, so once a month we would get on the 23 bus and pass through East India Dock Road. But what memories! Of triumph and tragedy, of human warmth and kindness and the hard realities of life. And the characters – boy do I miss them! Talk about a slice of life.

South of Cable Street was considered a 'no go' area for us. Occasionally, when visiting Watney Market (now that was a market) with my mother, we would reach the end of Watney Street and I would glance across Cable Street and wonder. Then when I was older my uncle occasionally took me for a walk through the docklands areas 'south of Cable Street'. I wondered how he knew where he was going, but after reading your book I think I now know. As a gambler and an unmarried womanizer I think he visited some of the establishments that you describe!

As I was reading your book I thought 'she is the James Herriot of the East End in the fifties – they could make a television series out of this material.' When I looked you up on your publisher's website, this is exactly what persuaded you to write your book!

I wondered why you never mentioned any encounters with Jewish residents of the area. However, when I thought about it I realized why. Those were not the days of 'interfaith dialogue'. For Jews there was always the danger of attempts to convert us to the Christian religion. From the places my forbears had come from this was a great danger and therefore the community looked after itself, and while the C of E was seen as relatively benign, the Catholic Church was not! My mother used to tell me how, when she was a girl in the twenties, the mission on Sutton Street would offer buns if you came inside to listen to the preacher. She used to go in for the buns! While she did not believe much in religion she was not going to be persuaded to convert to anything else! So in reflecting on your book I realized that the last thing a Jewish woman would want would be a delivery arranged by Nonnatus House.

Your appendix covering the Cockney dialect was superb. I used to speak with a broad Cockney accent until I was 16. At Grammar School in the sixties, you realized that unless you learnt to speak 'proper' you would not get very far in life and in particular out of the East End. My father used to drive me crazy because he would always say *hisn* (he pronounced it *heesn*) instead of 'his'. I used to say to him '*hisn* isn't a word!' Now I understand that my father spoke to me in Tudor English! If he was alive for me to tell him he wouldn't understand!

I can't thank you enough for writing about your memories. Those days have gone forever, but for those of us who experienced them they will live forever. As I get older I find myself going back to them, thinking of the richness of the experiences and the drama of daily life at the time. I realize that my wife, who is American, quietly understands some of the relics of Cockney that remain in my vocabulary even though I haven't explained them to her (like 'being in a right two and eight'

(2/8)). I sometimes realize it and ask 'do you know what that means?' and she gives me a soft look and says 'I worked it out'.

Please continue to write. I was sitting with my wife yesterday in a very sedate doctor's waiting room on the Upper East Side reading your book and in trying to suppress my laughter I started rocking from side to side until I just had to burst out laughing. (It was after Sister Julienne took the service after the pig was serviced – in reading the service every line seemed to refer to what she had just seen!)

Once again, many, many thanks for your efforts.

Yours very sincerely,
Bruce D. Godfrey

Bruce Godfrey now lives in the USA and adds:

In one of my other letters to Mrs Worth, in response to her telling me that her book was being turned into a series for the BBC, I made the comment, 'We will never see it here, it is much too local a subject to be screened here even on public television.' How wrong I was, something which I was very happy about!

Dear Jenny,

I bought your book from the post office a short time ago and very much enjoyed reading it. Being an old fogey, I can relate very well with that period. My mother had all her babies at home here during the 1920s attended by a midwife and our family Dr, Dr Young. As you mention, any males in the family were kept well away.

Hot water had to be boiled and our toilet was a very primitive affair in the back garden. Not a place to linger very long, when one's backside was exposed to a cold east wind.

Dr Young lived roughly on the top side of Horsecroft Road at the Fishery Road end.

During the war, we sat in his surgery waiting room, a conservatory adjoining the house. We waited our turn in total darkness with no heating and I should think any frail, elderly patient had a good chance of catching pneumonia.

Incidentally, Dr Young removed my appendix when I was a teenager although he was in fact, an eye specialist!

Living in that period would seem to be a hard life today but we were a happy family and knew of no other lifestyle.

Your Mrs Jenkins and the Irish girl, Mary, were not so fortunate.

We wish you and your family, a very happy Christmas and we look forward to your next book.

Brian

I'm busy reading your book and being a midwife and nurse, I enjoyed it even more. My earlier years have been nothing to compare with yours. I was in my late 20s before practising nursing in Switzerland.

Love from Elisabeth

In a later letter to her friend Elisabeth, Jennifer wrote about her love of music and singing:

I have always been a frustrated musician. Piano lessons as a child helped, but could not fulfil my longing . . . Singing was my passion (soprano) and at the age of 38 I gained a Licentiate of the London College of Music. Ten years later I was also elected an approved Fellow of the LCM. It was far too late to become a professional singer, but I sang and taught piano and singing for twenty-five years. My voice has almost gone now but I can still sing in choirs, and do so all over England and Europe. It is a great joy.

Dear Jennifer,

I heard an interesting story today of an old lady who had 3 strokes and was not expected to survive. Her daughter was reading *Call the Midwife*, and when she discovered that her mother could read, she encouraged her. She fixed up a reading stand for her and left your book propped up. She was astonished to see a rapid improvement. The result was her mother's discharge home!! She finished the book and was delighted to tell of her own experiences of childbirth 70 years ago!!

I understand that she puts her rapid recovery to the determination to finish the book!!

I am enclosing a small plaque which belonged to my mother who worked as a maternity nurse before she was married so it must be just over 100 years. I hope you will enjoy having it.

Sincerely,
No.1 Fan!
Ann Cowper

Dear Mrs Worth,

Having just read your book, *Call the Midwife*, the memories of my early childhood came flooding back. I congratulate you on a book written so truthfully and yet conveying what it was like to live in that area and in such appalling conditions. I was born in 1942 and would have been a true Cockney if the nasty Luftwaffe had not damaged Bow Bells. Although I was an only child, my father, whose family had arrived in the East End with the Huguenots, had 7 brothers and 6 sisters (or was it the other way round?). We lived in a number of locations, usually of the 'potty under the bed, one cold water tap and the "lav" at the end of the balcony' variety.

We catered for the overflow of children by sleeping three, sometimes four, to a bed. There were no locked doors. We used to run in and out of each other's houses. Discipline was applied impartially to all the kids by all the 'grown ups'. The sense of community was terrific.

One of my memories was standing guard over a large, heavy bike belonging to the midwife who visited one of my aunts during her pregnancy. Whilst visiting us, she would leave her bike in the courtyard. One afternoon my dad had come walking past and found somebody removing the bell. He'd immediately given said lad such a belt round the head it's a wonder it didn't come off!! About six of us were then detailed to stand guard on the bike for all subsequent visits by that lady. She was in the habit of patting one on the head as she collected her machine, rather heavily I remember, whilst addressing some familiarity to me in thanks. One day I went in and complained to my dad that the top of my head was being flattened. I was told under *no* circumstances was I to complain to her about this otherwise my 'bonts' really would be flattened right down to my ankles!! My father was fascinated by her in the nicest possible way, due I think to her accent. She radiated an aura of 'wonderful natural good humour', everybody in the building had a great respect for her. If my memory serves me correctly, it was the size of her hands that impressed me the most. Would it be the Chummy lady you refer to in your books? If so (and if she is still alive), please give her my regards and my admiration for the wonderful work that she and the rest of you midwife ladies did, who coped so well in such dreadful smog. I can remember sitting in the yard and not being able to see my hand when I stretched my arm out. My daughter doesn't believe this.

Thank you for reading this, Mrs Worth. I hope that you find it of some interest.

Regards,
Pete Williams

ps: I now live in a three-bedroomed cottage with living, dining rooms, etc., next to the Old Course, a palace compared to where I started my life. I still feel 'guilty' sometimes as I enter my home. Childhood circumstances never really fade do they.

Some memories of working in Poplar in 1956
by Edith Fox (née Horton)

After training as a general nurse in King's College Hospital, 1951–1955, I then trained as a Part 1 midwife at the British Hospital for Mothers and Babies in Woolwich for 6 months. I then went on to the Community of St John the Divine (CSJD) – then known as the Nursing Sisters of St John the Divine (NSSJD) – in the East of London, Poplar, for Part 2 midwifery training. I felt very privileged to do this with the CSJD Sisters because we also had experience of nursing 'on the district' (general nursing in the local area). Moreover, this was one of only four midwifery training places with this experience, i.e. not in a hospital. It was very important to me because I was hoping to go to East Africa to work with the Anglican missionary society, UMCA – later known as USPG. I did in 1958.

I arrived at the mission house in Ladore Street, Poplar, complete with a very heavy Raleigh sit-up-and-beg bicycle which had belonged to my aunt. It was extremely heavy and unwieldy! I was greeted by Sr Margaret Faith who said, 'Oh dear! You are a large lady and I haven't got a uniform to fit you!' So after a cup of tea and cake in the kitchen she hurried off to the Co-op nearby and purchased for me two dark-blue men's overalls. They fitted except that they were much too short, so I needed to wear a suitable skirt underneath. I felt very different and odd, but in the end it didn't seem to matter very much.

The others in the group were Jo Willoughby and Comfort Oku. Jo and I resumed our friendship some years ago. Comfort was a Nigerian-trained nurse whose mother was matron of a maternity hospital in Nigeria and needed Comfort to be fully trained in order to help her. Comfort was a lovely, jolly plump African who wasn't too fond of work! She couldn't ride

197

a bicycle and had no intention of doing so. She walked to the bus stop and soon learnt all the necessary bus times and routes. In an emergency Sr Miriam would take Comfort to deal with a patient in her small black Austin 7, which we called 'Phoebe'. Sr Miriam was disabled, but always had a smile and showed great courage in climbing up to the 18th floor of Peabody Buildings, if she had to. The lifts seldom worked! So Comfort was usually assisted with her patient visits by Sr Miriam. Sr Margaret Faith, the Sister Superior of the house, always seemed to be in a great hurry. She often cooked our main meal, as well as working on the district. There were also two lay sisters who looked after the roof garden, where they grew tomatoes and other vegetables. It was a great joy to us all to sit up there in the sun in our off-duty times and admire the flowers and vegetables.

The trained midwife who looked after me was Susan Cutter (née Thomas-Davis). On one occasion we found ourselves having to deliver an undiagnosed breech presentation. The GP couldn't come – being very involved elsewhere, so we got on with it and fortunately a lovely baby was safely delivered and all was well. These unexpected emergency challenges luckily didn't happen very often!

Once a week we cycled through the Greenwich Tunnel, which was a cycle track and walkway parallel to the Blackwell Tunnel, and took us to Deptford on the other side of the river. We went to the Sisters' house there for lectures by Sr Madeline, and then cycled back to Poplar in time for a cup of tea.

The communities of Poplar and the Isle of Dogs were poor but extremely warm-hearted people and very loveable. They all helped one another as much as possible, especially those living in the slummy high-rise apartments of Peabody Buildings. During the early 1950s it was the height of fashion to own a cocktail cabinet, complete with patterned glass doors. They were very modern, but most families used them to house all the baby clothes and nappies, and everything needed for a new baby. So we always knew where to find a spare nappy when needed! Sometimes it was necessary for us to spend a few hours with the patient waiting as labour progressed and neighbours or husband offering cups of tea. We called it 'stimulised' tea, because it was made from very stewed teabags with sterilised milk or even condensed milk and lots of sugar. It tasted horrible even if it helped to keep us awake! After all this tea drinking, we sometimes needed to use the toilet. This was usually outside, with a door that didn't fit – on one occasion I was shown a toilet with a very battered door that was completely useless. It was most embarrassing to sit there knowing that the family could see you from the house! Once, while visiting in a very slummy house, I was offered two fried eggs on a tin plate that looked as if it had never been washed up. But I ate them to keep me going, and prayed that I would survive. I did.

The men of the families worked in the Docks when work was available. Sometimes they, having a very large family of 15 or more children, were better off on the 'dole'. I helped deliver the 16th child of one such family. The father did not work but helped look after the family. They kept one very small room especially for mum and the new baby with a single bed in it, plus the cocktail cabinet. The rest of the family somehow all crowded into the other room. But the children were always well fed, not so well clothed, and the toddlers were always running around with bare bottoms, being potty-trained – to save on nappies.

We joined the Sisters in chapel for Compline as often as we could. On Sunday mornings, some of us went to All Saints' Parish Church for the Communion Service. On Christmas Eve, we all went to Midnight mass. I asked Sr Margaret Faith: 'What about the patients ringing up?' She told me that St John would look after them all – which I found reassuring! Some of us got to know the clergy of the parish quite well . . . There was a large vicarage next to the church which housed a vicar and usually 6 curates. They usually came to the parish dances in the church hall, and if Susan and I were off duty we always went. They were great fun and a welcome time of socialising and meeting different people.

After I qualified as a midwife I did a 4-month theatre course in Kent and then went to the missionary training College of the Ascension in Selly Oak, Birmingham. I was at the College for a year, but during the long holiday times I returned to the Sisters in Poplar to help out with the work on the district. I was there for part of Lent, when on Fridays we ate salt fish for our main meal. I found this very difficult to eat until I discovered that if you held your breath while swallowing a mouthful you did not taste it!

I was quite often given the early morning insulin run – 6 a.m. I met a lot of interesting people during these holiday times and got to know them well. One man always had clean sheets of newspaper on his table, a very small saucepan ready with water to boil up the syringe for the insulin, and a warm smiling welcome. We had some stimulating conversations while I lit his fire and made us a cup of tea. His daughter lived nearby and called in after my visit to make him breakfast and tidy up.

I had always hoped that eventually I would be able to join CSJD as a Sister, but while working in Tanzania I learnt that God had another plan for me – when I met my future husband there!

Dear Jennifer Worth,

Shadows of the Workhouse

Please forgive me for writing to you 'out of the blue'.

I have just finished reading your excellent book, and felt I must write to you personally. I expect you have received many letters on the book from ex-residents of the Isle of Dogs, and this is just another!

I married a girl from 195 Manchester Road. She lived there with her parents and her brother until their home was destroyed in April 1940. We have been married for 59½ years, and have 2 children, son 57 and daughter of 52.

Our daughter took her on a 'tour' of the area some years ago and she had difficulty in recognising anything in the Isle of Dogs. You obviously knew the district very well.

We met one another when we both worked for the post office; she was a telephonist, in the days prior to BT, and I was a trainee engineer. After the bombing, her family moved to New Malden in Surrey, where her brother, aged 89, still resides.

We both have had strokes! and she suffers from aphasia, very irritating for the sufferer, and difficult for her listeners. I have read large amounts of your marvellous book to her. She remembers the Swing Bridge (page 12)! but cannot remember any Convent. Your Nonnatus pseudonym? Perhaps you would kindly enlighten her please?

We had a friend who lived in Seaford (Sussex) and he wrote a book titled *Not Like Other Boys*, a story of his life, brought up by very devout Salvation Army parents *and* grandparents, and he served on a warship on 13 Russian convoys. Sadly it changed his way of thinking on life. He received *many* letters about his book, so I apologise if you find this one too much!

We are both 83 years of age and hope this missive is not too irritating for you!

Yours very sincerely,
M. J. Vicary

Jennifer wrote in her reply:

Thank you for writing to me, it was very kind of you and I appreciate it. It is so interesting to hear from people who lived in the area and I must have passed 195 Manchester Road many times. But like your wife, I don't recognise it any more, it is so changed. But the swing bridge is a very persistent memory, for it nearly killed me once!!! The convent was in Lodore street off the East India Dock Road, and the house is still there – but divided into flats now. Perhaps [your wife] remembers the 'Sisters in Blue' as the local people called them?

Dear Sirs,

I have just finished listening to the CD recordings of *Shadows of the Workhouse*, after listening to *Call the Midwife*, written by Jennifer Worth and read by Annie Aldington. Both of which I found to be excellent and after completing the first story I was compelled to listen to the next recording.

These stories fill you in with the history of times gone by and how difficult life was during such times. Museums show you buildings and give you an insight to how the people lived then, but certainly not the feeling and the struggles of everyday folk, particularly the poor. We take so much for granted these days with the National Health and the Benefit system, that it is beyond us now to ever consider life without them. Because of these stories the older people should certainly be assessed as a generation much stronger than the youngsters of today as these stories cover what they went through just to survive.

I was born just after the war and I lived with my grandmother who had 10 children herself. I thought I had an insight to life gone by, but these stories proved to be an eye-opener. I now realize how ignorant I have been to life at the turn of the last century, and to the people who are still alive today despite their encounters. My great-grandmother died due to complications during childbirth, after giving birth to twins, the second twin being born an hour after the first baby's arrival.

I had twins myself a century later. The only one in the family to repeat having identical twins which were unexpected as only one baby was expected! I survived to tell the tale, yet people find it hard to believe that in 1966 they were overlooked during my pregnancy and labour.

My twins were born at home because up until then if your

first arrival was born without problems at the hospital, then you were not considered to be at risk, which is what happened to me. I had moved into an area new to me which consisted of old terraced houses, occupied mainly by people who had lived in the area until old age, but because we had a bathroom I was assessed as not needing any extra care, despite me stating I felt that there were problems with my pregnancy. My normal weight in the 1960s was 8 stone, and I was told that this second baby of mine would probably be bigger than my first, as this was usual. When the baby was born I was told yes, this baby is bigger than your first child of 6 lb 4 oz, she looks nearer 7 lb. The midwife thought her job was complete until there was a splash of water and a backside appeared. Only then was it realized another baby was on the way. The undetected twins weighed in at 6 lb 12 oz and 6 lb 4 oz so altogether I had been carrying 13 lb of baby! My second twin quickly came into the world, and she arrived via a breeched delivery. Yet no further complications, only the shock to us all!

Women are still dying due to childbirth today with all our present-day technology, so how did women live through these encounters then? The stories should be made into films. Maybe then people will begin to appreciate the old and just how far we have come from these tales of hardship to the present-day assistance which is at hand now.

Could you please pass on my congratulations to Jennifer Worth for me and ask her why she decided to write these stories?

I hope to hear from you in the near future, but until then my eternal thanks go to all concerned for the story's output.

Yours faithfully,
Joan Lawrence (Mrs)

27 August 2008

Dear Jennifer,

I just had to write and say how much I have enjoyed reading your most moving books *Call the Midwife* and *Shadows of the Workhouse*.

I was born in 1944 so I can remember the 50s when I trained as a GPO telephonist at 16 in London, where the Barbican now stands was a massive bomb crater and also behind the Guildhall another bomb site.

My parents used to take my brother and I to see the ships unload in the Pool of London.

Another favourite of ours was Petticoat Lane market and all the coster stallholders selling china, curtains and the man with his monkey who used to sell pills and potions.

Best of all Brick Lane market where they used to sell pets – dogs, puppies and birds.

Thank you so much for such a wonderful read in these two books, which I will read again and again.

Yours sincerely,
Joan Myers

Joan Myers writes of her time as a telephonist:

It was by sheer chance that I became a General Post Office (GPO) telephonist. My father saw a recruitment advert for the GPO and thought it a good, secure and pensionable Civil Service job for a sixteen-year-old.

I had my interview at Waterloo Bridge House, where they tested our hearing, speaking voice and spelling. Also how high we could reach from a sitting position, as not all exchanges had low, automatic switchboards and there were some with very high, old manual switchboards. Having passed the interview, my six weeks of training started at the London Wall training school. Some London exchanges preferred to train their own staff, especially if they covered important sites such as Scotland Yard, the MOD, Buckingham Palace and the Stock Exchange.

After surviving those first six weeks, we were then allocated to the exchanges where we would finish our training, and which would become our permanent base. We were also instructed that if ever there were public transport problems, we were to walk to our nearest exchange – no taking a sicky!

I was sent to New Cross Exchange in Peckham. It was built in 1953 and is still standing, I believe. New Cross covered a similar area to the one Jennifer Worth was sent to: Elephant and Castle, Surrey Docks, Deptford, Bermondsey, Peckham Rye and Nunhead. Telephone exchanges were still part of the Civil Service and controlled by the Postmaster General, so there were libraries of rules and regulations in each exchange to cover every situation. There was no laughing and talking between the operators whilst on switchboard, eyes front at all times and no eating sweets! (There was a strict dress code – no trousers, jeans or mini-skirts, even though the public never saw us.)

Most exchanges were very social places. At Christmas time we had a party for underprivileged children and each child received a gift. We collected tinned and packet food to make Christmas parcels for hard-up families and pensioners. Engineers in their vans and anyone who had a car would drop these parcels off at addresses given to us by social services.

Night staff came from all walks of life – we had ex-policemen, ex-servicemen, carpet salesmen and a pastry chef. Our day staff were a mixed bunch too – an ex-ballet dancer, a diplomatic service widow, a magician's assistant and a telephonist from an oil tanker in the merchant navy!

It was a rewarding job in lots of ways – the operator was

the first point of contact, not like today where you have to go through umpteen options and you still don't get a human being to speak to!

21 October 2009

Dear Mrs Worth,

I was so pleased to hear from you. I didn't expect to receive a reply from the author herself. I enjoyed both your books. After reading *Shadows of the Workhouse*, I found it so moving. I couldn't get into another book for ages. I am writing down my own family history, but there are so many gaps. I have rheumatoid arthritis so I can't get about as I used to so I rely on the internet. My own grandchildren have no idea what it was like to be poor in the past. They are enjoying their lives and that's as it should be. Maybe one day they will be interested in reading about it. Whenever I start doing any research I can almost feel my ancestors encouraging me to continue before it's too late.

I will have great pleasure in waiting for your last book to come out in large print. I must say you have had a very interesting and compassionate life. Sorry I am writing to you in print but my handwriting gets almost illegible after a while.

My best wishes to you and thanks again,
Iris Green

Iris Green also had this memory of her grandmother after the war, before her house was demolished:

When we visited my grandmother after the war, her house had been badly damaged from the bomb that had fallen on nearby Single Street School. She was living downstairs because it was too dangerous to go upstairs. She was waiting to be rehoused. I thought she would be delighted to have a nice new flat with an inside toilet and a bathroom with hot and cold water but I could see she was really upset. She had lived in the

East End all her life and she dreaded moving away from her friends and neighbours. All the houses were demolished and the site is now part of Mile End Park.

Dear Jennifer Worth,

I just had to write to you as author of *Call the Midwife* and *Shadows of the Workhouse*.

I enjoyed the books so much and thank you for taking the time to write down your experiences of the East End of London.

I was born in Bow hospital so am your true Cockney, although being born in 1938 just before the Second World War started, my father Robert James Thomas (tug captain on River Thames) moved mum and I to the country, a village called Catmere End on the Essex/Cambridge border, before going to war where, I am glad to say, he returned home safe and sound to us.

I have recently read my parents' letters to each other during the war. I knew my parents were a happy couple but the letters blew me away and they have now been accepted at the Imperial War Museum, for research purposes, on disc.

Both Mum and Dad were brought up in Poplar.

My great-grandmother died in childbirth leaving my grandmother aged 12 years old to try to bring the family up.

On my father's side in Poplar, my Aunt Annie worked in the local nunnery with the nuns but never took her vows, so whether it was Nonnatus or whatever the place is called, I understand this is not the real name, I assume the place is still up and running.

I can just about remember Aunt Annie, probably up to the early 50s.

I still have a book she bought me, *If Jesus Came to my House*, a child's book all written in rhyme.

I wonder if you ever met her. I would like to know more about her and what she did.

I am 72 years old and have been doing my family history. When I lived in the East End after the war, I was a needlewoman for the 'House of Worth' in Grosvenor Street, London Mayfair, making many clothes for stage and screen, also for very rich families.

Do you have any connection with 'The House of Worth' with your matching surname?

Thank you again for your books. Mrs Jenkins will live with me forever, especially those toenails!

I have recommended your books to friends and family.

> Yours sincerely,
> Cherry Chapman

In her reply Jennifer wrote:

Thank you so much for your letter, just received. What a fascinating story you tell. I don't know if your Aunt Annie worked with my Sisters of St John the Divine at the Mission House – she might well have done. It is lovely to get letters like yours and it gives me a great thrill to know I bring back memories.

Cherry Chapman writes of her time spent working in London in the fashion trade:

It was an exciting time being in London's haute couture trade. I helped on and made some amazing clothes. Day dresses, tea gowns, ball gowns. (Debutantes' fathers wanted the best for their daughters, to make sure they married well and looked really beautiful at the Debs' balls.) Also stage clothes for leading ladies on the London stage.

The Ascot races were a very busy time, with ladies waiting downstairs to be dressed each day in their new outfits before going to the races. Then there were film and stage stars, titled ladies, very rich ones, princesses and the Queen.

I made my own wedding dress and all three bridesmaid dresses, to be like the rich and famous! Two in white otto-man, a corded fabric, and the dark-haired bridesmaid was in gold lamé. I carried yellow roses and white flowers, the white bridesmaids yellow roses, and the gold bridesmaid had white roses.

✦

Dear Mrs Worth,

Having had a career as a nurse 1949–2006, a friend thought I might be interested in reading one of your books *Call the Midwife*. I am writing to say how this brought back a flood of memories. I trained at 'The London' – went on to do midwifery in Brighton and Cambridge. I did private work – casualty – finally chose ophthalmics at Moorfields. Marriage and two children were fitted in between!

In your book, the most moving moments are the reminders of the hard life and poverty the East Enders suffered post-war. I remember bomb sites, the SMOG, etc.

One of our daughters is now a qualified nurse in Australia. As nursing in general has changed so much since our time, your book has prompted me to write down some of my memories, which may be of interest to Rachel. Will she believe that all new admissions had to have a bath, and head examined for nits – or that each day started at 8 a.m. with prayers!

I feel I was very fortunate to have a career which I found really interesting, right up to retirement at 63 years. I think it was the talk of the throughput of patients that made me decide it was time to go!

Again, thank you for your very real story telling – and best wishes.

Pat Wallbank

Jennifer empathised with Pat Wallbank's experience in her reply:

You have had a very long career, mine was only from '53–'73, and I left because resuscitation came in and I couldn't take it. Everything in nursing has changed beyond recognition, but so has society. Young people don't believe the conditions we worked in . . .

Pat Wallbank remarks:

How times have changed! Going to the London Hospital in 1949 straight from school – never having seen another naked body – nor a really sick person, I was ill prepared for the situations I had to deal with. No 'counselling' in those days – hopefully a sympathetic Ward Sister to understand one's distress.

Many of the patients came from outside London with 'unusual' conditions, requiring a long stay in hospital. As a nurse this meant one became connected with them over their time on the ward. This is in contrast with my own recent experiences. Meet your 'named' nurse on admission – never to see her again as she's off on study leave!

I have just spent time with an old nursing colleague who lives in Boston. I met her whilst doing training at Moorfields Eye Hospital. We went on to spend a year doing ophthalmics in the USA. We talked a lot about our fun times together. Both of us have had several spells in hospital in our old age and feel glad to be alive!

Dear Jennifer Worth,

Thank you so much for writing *Call the Midwife*.

I too worked at a hospital in Gloucester run by a religious society whose Mother House was in Deptford.

After this I did my General Training in Lewisham from 1942. What a change!

What struck me was that the bomb damage and slums were still there in the late 1950s. We were promised that the damage would be cleared up after the 1945 election. I saw the starting of the building of the prefabs.

When my son-in-law went to Cologne in 1953 he said that he was very surprised to see no bomb damage as he had where he lived in North London. What is more Cologne had been rebuilt.

I wonder if the patients laughed at your accent as they did mine as I came from rural Gloucestershire.

Thank you again for a most interesting and informative book – how I hated the tramlines when riding my bicycle!

Yours sincerely,
Betty M. Hayes

Betty Hayes' experiences in the war were published in the WI booklet What Did you Do in the War, Granny? *Here is a section from that essay*:

I left school in February 1940 to go to work as a nurse at the Children's Hospital in Gloucester, now no longer in use. There I saw rickets, paralysis from polio, diphtheria, scarlet fever, rheumatic fever, whooping cough, TB, meningitis, hare-lips and cleft palates, and malnutrition for the first time. The worst part was having to stop parents from visiting their children if the children cried. We had three hours off a day, half a day a week and one day off once a month. We were paid £12 per annum minus National Insurance.

After two years, at the age of 18, I went to do my General Training at St John's Hospital, Lewisham, which is now demolished. I arrived to find an enormous hole in the ground where a landmine had landed. My pay went up to £30 per annum I think, with one day off a week, three hours a day and four hours on Sunday. After three months I was transferred to British Legion Emergency Hospital near Maidstone. The wards were long with forty beds to a ward. There I saw malaria, colitis, soldiers with amputated legs, and sometimes we had a ward full of patients suffering from the effects of smallpox vaccinations. One man there sticks out in my memory. He had seen his two sons killed in front of him. He wouldn't eat and withdrew into himself. Obviously he was suffering from depression, but the doctor put him in 'jankers' and he used to be marched up and down the aisles separating the wards. It was not all work and no play there. We often went to dances at Maidstone, West Malling and Ashford barracks, as girls were in short supply.

After 9 months or so I was transferred back to Lewisham where the food was considerably better along with the living accommodation, although the rules were much stricter. Whilst there, I have fond memories of listening to Glenn Miller and his dance orchestra. I even danced to his music live. I danced at several palais, and was introduced to the ballet, which I loved.

Before D-Day I was told by Matron to be prepared to go overseas. I had to get a blanket from home and we would be issued with a kidney dish and instruments. We didn't go to France as there were not as many soldiers wounded as envisaged but many more were killed.

Not long afterwards the flying bombs, or doodle-bugs as we called them, started. I shall always remember the first night.

We thought that German bombers were being brought down by our fighters. After the doodle-bugs cut out there was silence and then a loud explosion as they landed. The nurses upstairs came down to us. They thought it was safer. Some slept on the floor and others shared beds with us. Matron came in. She was horrified. After that we had to sleep in the air-raid shelter.

One of the first doodle-bugs came down on Marks & Spencer's in Lewisham High Street, just as a bus was passing, taking girls to work. The glass of the bus shattered, blinding every one of them. We had a ward full of blind girls, many of them pregnant, with their husbands serving in France. It was terrible. They were about the same age as I was. I have often wondered what happened to them. All the waiting-list patients' operations were cancelled and we concentrated on air-raid casualties. The casualties were operated on and shipped to other hospitals in the country in converted Green Line coaches, each holding about seven beds.

After the doodle-bugs came the rockets. We had started ordinary operations by then. I was transferred to theatre work. After the daytime operations, we had to wash the walls ready for the casualties. At one time we had two operating tables in one theatre with three surgeons operating on one patient, one for the head, one for the trunk and one for the lower limbs. I well remember one morning going outside about seven a.m., having started at seven-thirty a.m. the previous day, to see a most spectacular sunrise. We went to bed in the shelter, but were woken up at ten-thirty to go on duty. We had been working so hard that Matron gave us one and a half days off. I went to stay with some friends near Crayford and couldn't sleep, so two of my family took me for a drink of whisky at a pub. One was a young Canadian rear-gunner. He was shot down and killed two days later.

Eventually things quietened down and VE Day arrived. Matron said we could go up to London after finishing work at

9 p.m. Crowds of people lined The Mall. Winston Churchill came on the balcony. We all shouted for the King to come onto the balcony, which of course he and his family did. I also heard a trumpet playing and afterwards realized it was Humphrey Lyttelton. I think some of the buildings were floodlit – what a marvellous sight. I had never seen anything like it before.

✦

Dear Mrs Worth,

Many thanks for your letter. I'm so pleased that you are writing another book – on my order list.

I didn't start nursing until I was 33 in 1956 (an accountant before) so things were not so draconian. I was considered a good influence and was given a room on the ground floor so I was constantly hauling nurses in through my window until I was warned to be careful by one of the junior night sisters. She was coming back by taxi in the early hours and the taxi driver said he'd help her over the back wall and I'd let her in through my window – she didn't snitch on me.

I went to Stoke Mandeville for 4 months and stayed for 4 years – became hooked. It was a shock to the system at first because it wasn't like a hospital – noisy, clean, but not terribly tidy with a few eccentrics – one sister stopped a train in its tracks because she'd missed the hospital bus into Aylesbury.

Margot Fonteyn's husband was there when I eventually became the night super and everyone was terribly envious because she and I had supper and breakfast together each evening. His brother told me she had decided to leave him before this happened but then felt it was her duty to care for him. He said this was *not* the result of a political argument (as was reported) but the wrath of an irate husband and that he was a notorious womaniser. She was a saint. There was a bullet still lodged in his brain and he was completely irrational.

There was another Irish sister called Maggie Murphy who ran a check-up ward with the help of a one-legged orderly. It was only for paraplegics who could look after their own bladder and bowels, make their own beds, etc.

They were a lot of rogues, mainly ex-forces – used to forging late passes, coming in drunk, generally playing havoc.

It was Poppa Guttman's round and he came in with various visiting doctors. The main points were covered by these men. X-rays on laps, beds perfect, urine bottle at side, men immaculate.

The first man held up his 5 X-rays to show the clean kidneys and bladder, told him his haemoglobin and blood count and then said, 'If you will excuse me, sir, I'm due at the workshops.' Smart salute and wheeled out and so it went on.

Poppa G. (as he was known) was beside himself with pride. 'Why am I the proudest man in the world?' he said. 'I have the best staff in the world and these hardworking diligent patients,' and so on.

Maggie had had enough. 'They are nothing of the sort,' she said, 'they are idle, drunken, lecherous,' etc., etc.

Now for it, I thought. Poppa was notorious for his temper and we waited for it to erupt. 'We are a democracy,' he said. 'Everyone is entitled to their own opinion.'

I moved on to an acute surgical ward, and then became a tutor. I moved on to post-basic training and ended up with courses at Mount Vernon, Harefield and Hillingdon hospitals.

I knew very little of these specialties of course, but had very experienced clinical teachers for each, so lectured very little.

I spent some time on the difficulties of keeping the patient *at rest* and finally ended by asking them what could affect it. They got all but the 5% difference between male and female, and finally one of them said I'd have to tell them. 'Alright,' I said, 'what about sex?' to which I got the reply, 'Doesn't that come under exercise?' I had a lot of fun with my students, who called me TIDDLER behind my back – as if I didn't know.

I hope I haven't bored you with my ramblings.

As I said, I'm looking forward to buying your new book.

Best wishes,
Audrey Davidson

12 July 2009

Dear Miss Worth,

Call the Midwife brought back vivid memories of my first teaching post at St Michael and All the Angels RC Primary School in Paradise Street, Rotherhithe.

Arriving on the first morning in September 1954 was a daunting experience. Half the class were absent 'opping in Kent; the building was Victorian and when my full class quota was present 37 boys and girls aged 9+ greeted me. 'Good mornin', Miss.' The desks were double, arranged in blocks of two down both sides of the classroom. The child against the wall had to climb over three children to reach his or her place. My desk was well placed by the big stove, kept red-hot by the caretaker. The classroom was the central one of three which entailed much 'passing through'.

The children were deprived in all the ways you describe so vividly but they were wonderful – generous, sparky, tolerant, so my memories are only happy ones. I was very West End, convent-educated and understood very little of what they said; they certainly did not understand me. The Headmaster, an Irishman and quite exceptional in every way, did a great job in helping me learn Cockney and in introducing me to the children. I loved your chapter on the language as I had not realized how much I had learnt and how much I still remember.

The families were admirable in so many ways, warm and embracing. I think we were respected in the same way as you nurses were. The families were large, Catholic and lived in The Buildings, fathers worked on the docks when they could, mothers cleaned the City offices. I used to thoroughly enjoy the morning bus ride from London Bridge to school being well entertained by the cheerful cleaners. They must have felt exhausted.

School dinners were ample and very good, all the children had them, paying on a sliding scale, many of them free. The dinner register caused me agonies – it was seldom correct – I was grateful to the Head, who always put it right without comment. We all looked forward to dinner time and the staff ensured that certain children had second helpings or even thirds if available. There was never any 'I don't like this', everything was wolfed down at top speed – they were hungry.

One of my strongest memories is of the school hall, a largish room where morning assembly was held. The focal point was a statue of the Virgin Mary, always decked with flowers. None of the children had even a window box, every flower had to be bought. I worked in a number of very privileged schools during my teaching career, but Rotherhithe was the only one which produced a bank of glorious flowers to lift our hearts as we started the day. The memory still brings tears to my eyes.

A couple of years ago I returned to the area to 'have a look'. I suppose in many ways it has improved but I felt that the heart and soul had gone. The new flats looked miserable and poorly built. Many of the families were rehoused in Kent and I can still hear around me the traces of the accents of those London days.

Your book has stirred my heart and reminded me of the wonderful school where the Head, the staff, the helpers, parents and children initiated me into a long and very, very happy teaching career. They did for me what your nuns and fellow nurses did for you.

Many thanks for re-awakening all those memories.

Yours sincerely,
Maria Lenko (Mrs)

Jennifer replied to Maria Lenko with what Maria describes as a charming letter, thanking me for my empathetic reaction to her book and suggesting that I should consider writing in greater detail about my experiences in education in the East End. She made the point that interest in social commentary on those years, before it was too late, was greater than ever.

Dear Mrs Worth,

Your book *Call the Midwife* was a complete joy. Having done the rounds on the bicycle in the late 50s, memories came flooding back.

I sent copies to two friends in the USA, the verdict was unputdownable. Rita was in Gloucestershire and she related this incident.

She was called out at 2 a.m. to a patient in labour. The pedal fell off her bicycle and the bedpan landed in the ditch. A man appeared with a shotgun. 'Don't shoot, don't shoot, I'm the nurse,' was Rita's cry. (Apparently his chickens had been stolen.)

He said, 'What are you doing down there?' She is now crying. 'My bedpan's in the ditch!' He took pity on her and took her, the bicycle and the bedpan in his truck to the patient's home.

Thank you for a delightful read.

Yours faithfully,
Joyce Wainwright

Joyce also recalls one delivery in Newcastle when the family pet, a greyhound, ran off with the placenta!

Jennifer wrote back, saying:

Thank you for your lovely letter. I adore the story about the pedal falling off the bike, and the man with a gun! What a situation!! We nurses and midwives had to be able to manage *anything*, and we did. What surprises me is that no one has written about us before. We were real adventurers!

Joyce Wainwright wrote back with a few more stories:

Dear Mrs Worth,

Thank you for your lovely letter. I am now waiting for *Shadows of the Workhouse* to appear in paperback to give to my friends as they all praised *Call the Midwife* to the heavens.

My great friend Jackie came from Yorkshire and her mother, the lovely Ruby, was the village midwife. One night she decided to take a short cut across a field to her labouring patient, she tripped over a recumbent cow and her midwifery pack was lost. She retraced her steps to the nearest house. The man of the house came with her carrying a flashlight and found the bag and escorted her to the patient. Following the delivery, the husband walked her back home.

Another time when the snow was on the ground, a man knocked on the door asking for the midwife as his wife was in labour. Jackie's father opened the window of the bedroom and told him that she was out and he had to ring the other midwife. 'I haven't got any money,' was his reply. Oscar threw down a few pennies which promptly sank in the snow. He must have been confused as the only phone in the village, besides the phone box, was the one in the midwife's house!

Here's wishing you a
Nadolig Llawen a Blwyddyn Newydd Dda,
Joyce Wainwright

＊

Just after Jennifer's last book, In the Midst of Life, *was published, she discovered she had cancer. With characteristic fortitude and wisdom, she accepted her condition and, in her own words, 'accepted it as part of life'. She said, 'I feel that everything is slipping away from the periphery, which is rather nice . . . As everything slides away, what I am left with is faith and love. Faith, which has been the cornerstone of my life, and love, which has always been with me. Love of my husband; our love for each other; love of my daughters and my grandchildren, and their surpassing care of me. And overall, and around all, the love of God. Thanks be to God.'*

Jennifer Worth died in May 2011, but her legacy remains.

✦

*Music was a lifelong passion for Jennifer. In the 1970s, she embarked
on her second career, taking refresher piano lessons with Jackie
Chapling. On hearing of Jennifer's diagnosis, Jackie and her husband wrote to her: Sadly the letter arrived too late and Jennifer
never saw it.*

29 May 2011

Dear Jennifer,

I have only just heard that you are extremely ill with cancer. It
seems such a short while since I wrote to congratulate you on
your wonderful book *In the Midst of Life*. I am sure that your
very positive feelings about death will remain steadfast so that
you will have nothing to fear. You have lived such an interesting life with three separate careers as well as that of a wife and
mother of course. You left the best until the end. Most of us
feel pleased if we can give pleasure to a few people during our
lives, but in your very successful stories about your midwifery
experiences in the East End of London, you have reached out
and given pleasure to hundreds of thousands, perhaps even
more!

With love and affection,
Jackie and Michael Chapling

✦

The author of this letter did not realise that Jennifer had died. It was forwarded to the family by the publisher some months later.

November 2011

Dear Jennifer,

I have been meaning to write for a while, as I wanted to express my delight in, and gratitude to you for, your book *In the Midst of Life*. I have to confess I finished reading it in September but having never written to an author before, have procrastinated in writing to you.

I am a cancer nurse at the Royal Marsden Hospital where I have worked for eighteen years in a variety of roles, currently as a Matron. Throughout my career as a nurse I have always admired those who keep their focus on the essence of patient care whilst also embracing advancements and change in healthcare. I have looked up to a fair few role models in my time but have never felt so privileged to be a nurse or inspired to make a difference as I felt after reading your book. To me you truly capture the heart of nursing and at a time when there is lack of certainty in healthcare and disagreement about the focus of nursing, it was a real gift to read.

You have really challenged my thinking about resuscitation and reminded me of the true value of dignity, something we talk much about (particularly in cancer care) but which in today's healthcare service, we rarely truly embrace. Your honest account of your experiences as a junior nurse on a cancer ward and when you had more authority as a Ward Sister are moving, funny and most of all thought-provoking. I was at times in tears but was glad to be as I appreciated your concerns and passions about the way in which we treat those at the end of their life.

Thank you so much for sharing your experiences and writing with such warmth and depth, it has made a huge difference to the way I feel about nursing and has encouraged me immensely.

I hope this finds you comfortable despite your 'slipping away from the periphery' and I hope and pray too that the faith and love that you reflect so well in your book remain as bold as ever in the life you have left.

With much gratitude,
Kind regards,
Caroline Law

Jennifer's daughter, Suzannah, wrote back to Caroline Law to inform her of the sad news that Jennifer had passed away. She received the following in reply:

22 February 2012

Dear Suzannah,

I just had to write to express my delight in the BBC series of 'Call the Midwife', which has sadly just finished. Following your lovely reply to my letter written to your mother in response to her incredible book, *In the Midst of Life,* I wanted to add my gratitude to those of many other viewers for the wonderful TV adaptation of your mother's first three books about her time as a midwife in the East End. I am so pleased it has been so well received and I hope it has helped ease the pain for you of losing her back in May.

Your mother's memoirs have obviously touched the heart of the public and it has really encouraged me to know that the stories of her incredible, yet everyday experiences have been captivating to so many.

For me, it has been particularly wonderful as I feel I have been watching someone I know, even though I never of course met Jennifer! Having related to her thoughts and opinions about cancer care and the care of the dying in her last book however, it has been really interesting to get to know the younger, naïve Jennifer when she first started out as a community midwife. She obviously faced a world that was completely alien to her relatively comfortable upbringing in Amersham, but her wisdom, honesty and strength of character portrayed in the TV series shine through early on.

Thank you so much for your personal response to my first letter, it meant a great deal. I hope you now receive many letters of praise via the BBC about the TV series, and I hope too that you and your family are really happy with how your mother's life has been portrayed and can feel proud on her behalf.

Many, many thanks again,
Caroline Law

✦

Dear Philip, Suzannah & Juliette,

Thank you Suzannah for sending the information about the concert in June in memory of Jenny. I had been going to write in any case to let you know how much we have enjoyed watching *Call the Midwife* – along with so many other people. Amazing the number watching it. Also we have read with great interest the *Radio Times* 3 articles related to that. They have done remarkably well – even if a few things didn't really tally with my own experience in Poplar at the time!

I was so interested to read your own contributions to those articles and it is so lovely to see the photograph of dear Sister Jocelyn with you as a child, Suzannah, at Hastings. I also worked for 2 months earlier in the 50s at Hastings – so knew of the caravan too! I've been in touch with the Sisters at Birmingham and I'm told they have been asked to give some help with the next 8 episodes early next year. So it all goes on . . . !

Quite a legacy your dear wife, mother and grandmother has left and maybe even in excess of what she herself might have thought. I also owe much to my time with the Nursing Sisters and to District Midwifery both in London's East End and also in the similar slums of Glasgow where I did my Part II Midwifery with the Queen's District Nurses (which no longer exist sadly).

It was wonderful to be in touch with Jenny again through reading *Call the Midwife* and recognising her maiden name! Such a privilege in view of all that has happened since. So many people here are intrigued that I was there in Poplar at the same time and knew Jenny. They have been avidly watching everything and quizzing me about them! I have so loved seeing these Sisters in the exact same religious habits they wore then and so well played by those actresses.

The pupil midwives I took out on cases I remember very well and have been in touch with since. It was such a very fulfilling life we lived. All so changed now. Did you see amongst Jenny's things the article by Diana Lukeman in the *Nursing Times* called 'Barges, Bridges and Babies'? Diana was a pupil too at the same time.

With love to you all
and with our prayer and all best wishes,
Nancy & John

Dear Mr Worth,

Please accept my condolences on the loss of your wife, and my apologies for intruding at this time.

I have never written 'fan mail' in my life, but intended to write to Jennifer, after reading her midwife trilogy, to thank her for 'fleshing out' my family background.

She wrote of life in the East End of London in the 1950s. My parents were born in 1902 and 1907 in South Kensington and Herne Hill, but had married and moved to the south long before I was born in 1944, so I know very little of the lifestyle of my grandmothers. (Both died in their early 60s, again, long before my birth.)

Jennifer's account gave me a much-appreciated insight into the hardships they survived, and also why the 'poor house' was sometimes referred to by my parents, as a place to be avoided at all costs.

(I did know my maternal grandmother had to carry water up three flights of stairs, when her children were young. And also that she once 'took gunpowder' to cause a miscarriage. My mother had been sent to buy ½d-worth from the ironmonger 'to put on the fire, to clean the chimney' – she must have been desperate!)

Last summer, I bought *In the Midst of Life* – and that spoke so powerfully to me, that I determined to write to Jennifer then. I googled and found her obituary. I was only halfway through the book at the time, so that news came as a shock – almost like losing a friend.

That book made me realise how privileged we were, that I was able to care for both our mothers at home with us until their deaths. I found the book such compelling reading, and so thought-provoking, that I have passed it on to our recently ordained lady curate to read. I think it should be on the reading list for all doctors and clergy.

Again, please forgive my intrusion, but I hope you and your daughters will find some comfort in the knowledge that Jennifer's books are, I think, *important* works.

I am pleased to see they are to be televised.

Yours sincerely,
Carol Pigott

Dear Mr Worth & Family,

In the last few weeks I have read with the greatest pleasure several of Jennifer's books.

I have recently just finished *In the Midst of Life* and then having gone to the internet, discovered that Jennifer died at the end of May this year.

I am sure you miss her hugely and yet it seemed very much God gave her that 'quiet night and perfect end' she so wanted for others and herself.

I trained as a nurse and health visitor. Jennifer's care for people and her ability to catch life in all its quirkiness, pathos and joy, moved me to tears several times as I read.

In the Midst of Life moved me on in discussing an end of care life plan for my 95-year-old mother. She moved to a lovely care home, longing that she too will have a 'quiet night and perfect end'.

I so hope this letter reaches you all.

With very best wishes,
Claire Ball (Mrs)

✦

*On hearing of Jennifer's death, Paul Jennings – the biker – wrote
again, this time to the family:*

14 September 2012

In 2009 I discovered Jennifer's work in the form of *Shadows of
the Workhouse*, eagerly followed by the two other books in the
trilogy. I was so affected by Jennifer's amazing true stories that
for the first time in my life I was moved to write to an author.
Imagine my delight when I received a handwritten reply, which
is now a cherished possession.

As soon as *In the Midst of Life* was published, I purchased
a copy. I did not start reading it straight away – life and work
just got in the way. It was upon hearing the shocking and very
sad news of Jennifer's untimely death that I started to read the
book. The book was just as good as I had expected it to be,
further enhancing my respect for a wonderful life well lived.
However, I was quite unprepared for the last paragraph of the
last chapter 'Last Thoughts' which I read through tears.

I just wanted to let Jennifer's family know that she has
touched the soul of many of her readers, most of whom she
never met. I am sure your family's hearts must be bursting with
pride at her amazing life and achievement.

Kind regards,
Paul Jennings

Dear Paul

The Late Jennifer Worth

Thank you so much for your letter dated 14th September 2012, which arrived via the publisher just a few days ago. I am the eldest of Jennifer's two daughters and your letter (and the copy of the letter sent to my Mother in 2009) compelled me to reply.

Your letter of 2009 was one that I had recently read, so it came as no surprise. When my Mother died, there was a huge amount of paperwork to go through and in doing so I discovered that she had kept every one of the letters she received over the years from her 'fans'. There are countless letters; too many to have read them all, but yours was one that stood out. Something about it struck me; I don't know what. Maybe it was the image of a 6 foot, 14 stone biker, trained in martial arts, being reduced to tears of sadness. Or maybe it was simply that the letter was so well written.

Our lives have changed completely since her death, as I am sure you can imagine, but surprisingly, some of the changes are positive: My Father, Philip and I find ourselves being asked to give talks about Jennifer and her writing. It was at one such talk recently that I read out a number of letters and yours was one of the letters I selected most especially, for the reasons given above. It gives us enormous pride and pleasure to talk about her, and in a funny sort of way, keeps her memory alive for us.

I am so glad that you kept the letter she sent you and that it is a treasured possession. Her original writing is definitely something to be valued.

Your recent letter struck me still further. Her 'Last Thoughts' really were her last thoughts, dictated and transcribed in the last weeks of her life. She knew she was going to die and she was prepared for it. Such was her courage in facing her own death it gave us courage, and we found we could face it calmly too.

Suzannah Hart